Mariano Zelke

Algorithms for Streaming Graphs

Mariano Zelke

Algorithms for Streaming Graphs

Approaching Graph Problems with Limited Memory and without Random Access

Südwestdeutscher Verlag für Hochschulschriften

Impressum/Imprint (nur für Deutschland/ only for Germany)
Bibliografische Information der Deutschen Nationalbibliothek: Die Deutsche Nationalbibliothek verzeichnet diese Publikation in der Deutschen Nationalbibliografie; detaillierte bibliografische Daten sind im Internet über http://dnb.d-nb.de abrufbar.
Alle in diesem Buch genannten Marken und Produktnamen unterliegen warenzeichen-, markenoder patentrechtlichem Schutz bzw. sind Warenzeichen oder eingetragene Warenzeichen der jeweiligen Inhaber. Die Wiedergabe von Marken, Produktnamen, Gebrauchsnamen, Handelsnamen, Warenbezeichnungen u.s.w. in diesem Werk berechtigt auch ohne besondere Kennzeichnung nicht zu der Annahme, dass solche Namen im Sinne der Warenzeichen- und Markenschutzgesetzgebung als frei zu betrachten wären und daher von jedermann benutzt werden dürften.

Verlag: Südwestdeutscher Verlag für Hochschulschriften Aktiengesellschaft & Co. KG
Dudweiler Landstr. 99, 66123 Saarbrücken, Deutschland
Telefon +49 681 37 20 271-1, Telefax +49 681 37 20 271-0, Email: info@svh-verlag.de
Zugl.: Berlin, Humboldt-University, Diss., 2009

Herstellung in Deutschland:
Schaltungsdienst Lange o.H.G., Berlin
Books on Demand GmbH, Norderstedt
Reha GmbH, Saarbrücken
Amazon Distribution GmbH, Leipzig
ISBN: 978-3-8381-0806-3

Imprint (only for USA, GB)
Bibliographic information published by the Deutsche Nationalbibliothek: The Deutsche Nationalbibliothek lists this publication in the Deutsche Nationalbibliografie; detailed bibliographic data are available in the Internet at http://dnb.d-nb.de.
Any brand names and product names mentioned in this book are subject to trademark, brand or patent protection and are trademarks or registered trademarks of their respective holders. The use of brand names, product names, common names, trade names, product descriptions etc. even without a particular marking in this works is in no way to be construed to mean that such names may be regarded as unrestricted in respect of trademark and brand protection legislation and could thus be used by anyone.

Publisher:
Südwestdeutscher Verlag für Hochschulschriften Aktiengesellschaft & Co. KG
Dudweiler Landstr. 99, 66123 Saarbrücken, Germany
Phone +49 681 37 20 271-1, Fax +49 681 37 20 271-0, Email: info@svh-verlag.de

Copyright © 2009 by the author and Südwestdeutscher Verlag für Hochschulschriften Aktiengesellschaft & Co. KG and licensors
All rights reserved. Saarbrücken 2009

Printed in the U.S.A.
Printed in the U.K. by (see last page)
ISBN: 978-3-8381-0806-3

to my wife

Contents

1 **Introduction**   5

2 **The Semi-Streaming Model**   9
    2.1 Discussion on the Per-Edge Processing Time 9

3 **Related Work**   11

4 **Optimal Per-Edge Processing Times**   15
    4.1 Introduction 15
    4.2 Computing Certificates and Buffering Edges 16
        4.2.1 Connected Components 18
        4.2.2 Bipartition 18
        4.2.3 k-Vertex Connectivity 19
        4.2.4 k-Edge Connectivity 20
        4.2.5 Minimum Spanning Forest 20
    4.3 Closure 21

5 **Weighted Matching**   23
    5.1 Introduction 23
    5.2 The Algorithm 24
    5.3 Approximation Ratio 27
    5.4 Closure 38

6 **Cuts in Graphs**   39
    6.1 Introduction 39
    6.2 Minimum Cut 40
        6.2.1 Intractability 40

		6.2.1.1 An Alternative Proof	42
	6.2.2	Calculating Small Minimum Cuts	44
	6.2.3	Approximating Large Minimum Cuts	44
	6.2.4	Approximating Medium-sized Minimum Cuts	47
	6.2.5	Generalization	48
6.3	Maximum Cut		48
	6.3.1	Intractability	48
	6.3.2	Approximating Maximum Cut	50
	6.3.3	Generalization	52
6.4	Closure		53

7 Conclusion   **55**

Bibliography   **57**

Chapter 1

Introduction

> *"He had long ago concluded that he possessed only one small and finite brain, and he had fixed a habit of determining most carefully with what he would fill it."*
>
> ANNIE DILLARD, The Living

Today's computational tasks are facing an increasing amount of data. Oceanographic and atmospheric information is processed for climate prediction; IP traffic data is analyzed for billing purposes and to maintain network services. The volume of such massive data easily reaches terabytes or even petabytes. The particle physics experiment at the large hadron collider of CERN [CER] will soon produce data of a size of 15 petabytes per year [LHC] corresponding to more than 28 gigabytes on average every minute. That data is partly inspected in real-time but is also stored for later investigation.

In the traditional RAM model, c.f. [AHU75], an algorithm is assumed to be equipped with a memory that includes the whole input and allows fast random access to it. Every data item is within reach in no time at all.

These powerful assumptions are unreasonable for computational tasks as the above ones. Massive input data goes beyond the bounds of common main memories; thus, it is stored on disks or even tapes. Seek times, that is, movements of read/write heads are now dominating the time to call up single data items, making random access impractical. Moreover, if observed phenomena must be considered in a real-time manner, there is no random access at all.

This is where *streaming algorithms* arrive on the scene. They drop the requirement of random access to the input. By contrast, the input is assumed to arrive in arbitrary order as an *input stream*. In addition, the working memory of a streaming algorithm is constrained to be small compared to the size of the input; hence, it does not allow to memorize the whole input stream.

Streaming algorithms are not only useful to process arising data in real-time without completely storing it. Moreover, they provide a reasonable framework for processing data that is stored on external memory devices. For developing time-efficient algorithms working on these storage components, it is reasonable to assume the input of the algorithm (which is the output of the storage device) to be a sequential stream. While tapes produce a stream as their natural output, the output rate of a disk drastically grows if its content is accessed sequentially in the order it is stored.

Apart from their usefulness in practice, streaming algorithms also provide new insights into computational problems. While there is a developed theory for algorithms with bounded working memory, see e.g. [Pap94], comparatively few is known about the combination of bounded memory with forbidden random access. Such new insights may change the way we tackle computational tasks even for small problem instances. As it turns out in Chapter 4, there are problems that can be approached by a streaming algorithm within the same time bounds as in the RAM model. As a result, the transfer of the problem instance from an external memory into the main memory *before* starting the computation can be omitted. Instead, the computation can take place *while* the instance is read from the external device.

The largest amount of previous work in the area of data stream algorithms is focused on streams comprising numerical values. On such streams statistical data like frequency moments [AMS96], norms [Ind06], histograms [GGI+02], and quantiles [CKMS06] are of interest as well as the most frequent items [MAA06]. A comprehensive overview on the field of numerical streams is given by Babcock et al. [BBD+02] and Muthukrishnan [Mut05].

However, plenty of the emerging data can be regarded as a graph. The *call graph* of AT&T, modeling the users as vertices and the telephone calls as edges between them, consists of 200 million edges for every single day [Par08]. Not only for troubleshooting and forecasting, structural knowledge of this graph is of great interest. It can also help to identify fraudulent behavior [CPV02].

An even bigger graph is the *web graph* whose vertices are the webpages, two of them joined by a directed edge if there is a hyperlink in between. The discovery of structural information about this graph is a streaming problem: Since there is no explicit storage of the web graph, there is no random access to it. Instead, vertices and edges are spotted by web crawlers, i.e, little software agents that move along hyperlinks and report them to a server. There are approaches to reveal the topology of the web graph [BAJ00] or to utilize the connectivity structure to detect emerging communities [KRRT99].

To handle graph issues in a streaming context, Muthukrishnan [Mut05] proposed the *semi-streaming model*: The input graph is presented as a stream of its edges in arbitrary order to a *semi-streaming algorithm*. The working memory of this algorithm is restricted to allow the storage of all vertices but only a polylogarithmic number of edges on average for every vertex. Hence, input graphs that are too dense cannot be stored completely within the working memory. To find space-efficient summarizations for such graphs according to the query to be answered, is the challenge for a semi-streaming algorithm.

This book is concerned with semi-streaming algorithms tackling different graph problems. Chapter 2 formally introduces the semi-streaming model and its parameters while Chapter 3 summarizes related work in the area of graph problems under streaming assumptions. Chapter 4 presents the results obtained in [Zel07] about optimal processing times for some basic problems on graphs and slightly extends these results for k-vertex and k-edge connectivity. The problem of finding a maximum weighted matching is the focus of Chapter 5 that covers results of [Zel08]. Chapter 6 investigates the possibilities to find minimum and maximum cuts in graphs. A conclusion of the whole book can be found in Chapter 7.

Each of Chapters 4-6 starts with an introductory section giving the necessary definitions as well as the related work and contains concluding remarks at its end. Provided the reader is familiar with the basic concepts of graph theory, cf. [Die05], and the formal definition of the semi-streaming model, cf. Chapter 2, every chapter is self-contained and should be coherent on its own.

Chapter 2

The Semi-Streaming Model

The semi-streaming model was coined by Muthukrishnan in 2003 [Mut05] to approach graph problems in the context of streaming.

Let $G = (V, E)$ be a graph on the vertex set V and the edge set E. We denote by $n = |V|$ and $m = |E|$ the number of vertices and edges, respectively. A sequence of the edges of G in arbitrary order we call a *graph stream*. A *semi-streaming algorithm* is presented a graph stream of G as the input. The algorithm's working memory is restricted to $\mathcal{O}(n \cdot \text{polylog}\, n)$ bits, where polylog n denotes $\log^s n$ for some constant s.

A semi-streaming algorithm may access the graph stream for P *passes*. Each pass starts at the beginning of the stream and goes over it in the same sequential one-way order. For all algorithms developed in this book, we have $P = 1$, that is, we are only concerned with algorithms that are content with a single pass over the input stream.

A key parameter of a semi-streaming algorithm is the *per-edge processing time* T. We define this to be the minimum time allowed between the revealing of two consecutive edges in the input stream. This definition of T renders the definitions of early papers more precisely; we give a discussion concerning that in Section 2.1.

After reading the whole graph stream, the algorithm might spend some time on postprocessing before giving an output. This *postprocessing time* is incorporated by the *computing time* which is defined as the total time from reading the first edge in the graph stream until the answer of the algorithm is computed.

Note that the space restriction of the model allows the storage of a polylogarithmic number of edges on average for every vertex. Hence, a graph with $\mathcal{O}(n \cdot \text{polylog}\, n)$ edges can be read entirely into the memory and treated in the postprocessing step. Such graphs are of no interest in this model since the intrinsic task for a streaming algorithm, that is, to make a space-efficient summarization of the input, becomes irrelevant. As a result, we will restrict our attention to graphs with $\omega(n \cdot \text{polylog}\, n)$ edges.

2.1 Discussion on the Per-Edge Processing Time

Early papers in the area of semi-streaming algorithms that consider the per-edge processing time T [FKM+05b; FKM+05a; Zel06] use T in an ambiguous way. While being used as the worst-case time to process a single edge on the one hand, it is equally used on the other hand, even if not explicitly stated, as amortized time charged over the number of edges. In fact, if tools as dynamic trees or disjoint set data structures are utilized, they give rise to amortized times since their time bounds are of amortized type as well. Processing the input edges is then assumed to be evenly spread over the whole computing time which is then assumed to be just $m \cdot T$.

This definition is not appropriate for a streaming algorithm: As pointed out by Muthukrishnan [Mut05] the computing time, i.e., the time to evaluate the property in question for items read in so far, is not the most important parameter of a streaming algorithm. What is more crucial is the maximum frequency of incoming items that can still be considered by the algorithm. That refers to the speed at which external storage devices can present their data content to a streaming algorithm and constitutes the frequency at which observed phenomena can be taken into account. To this aim it is desirable to maximize the potential rate of incoming items by postponing as much operations as possible to a moment after reading all input items, even at the cost of a higher computing time.

To model this worthwhile property of a streaming algorithm, we propose the definition of the per-edge processing time T to be the minimum allowable time between two consecutive edges in the graph stream. Note that, on the one hand, this notion is weaker than the idea of a worst-case time: It might be the case that on several edges in the input stream the algorithm has to spend a time longer than T, that is, the worst case time might be higher. But then edges arriving with a delay of T can be buffered while the algorithm processes a time-consuming edge.

On the other hand, such a buffer can only carry $\mathcal{O}(n \cdot \operatorname{polylog} n)$ edges and must be flushed regularly. Therefore, our definition of T is stronger than the notion of amortized time: The amortized notion allows the existence of edges whose processing is so time-consuming that succeeding edges overrun the buffer and cannot be considered by the algorithm. In contrast, our definition of T makes sure that a semi-streaming algorithm with that per-edge processing time is able to consider every single edge in a stream of edges arriving with a delay of T.

Chapter 3

Related Work

Since the work of Munro and Paterson [MP78] the area of streaming algorithms has become voluminous. In this chapter we give account to the work that has been done on graph problems in this area, i.e., where the input is composed of a graph's edges and the memory is too small to carry all of them. For a comprehensive overview on the other aspects in the area of streaming not considering graph problems, we again refer the reader to the surveys of Babcock et al. [BBD+02] and Muthukrishnan [Mut05] and the rich bibliography therein.

The paper of Henzinger et al. [HRR99] is the first one to examine graph problems in the context of streaming. In this paper it is proven that to test the k-vertex and k-edge connectivity for $1 \leq k < n$ and the planarity of a graph in P passes over the input requires $\Omega(n/P)$ bits of working memory. The same lower bound is presented for the problem of finding all the sinks of a directed graph together with an algorithm for it that achieves the lower bound. Moreover, it is shown that to estimate the number of edges in the transitive closure of a directed graph to within any constant factor in one pass requires a working memory of $\Omega(m)$ bits.

An early natural streaming algorithm covering a graph problem is given by Bar-Yossef et al. [BYKS02] approximating the number of triangles in a graph. The algorithm works in a randomized fashion and its space usage depends on the desired approximation ratio and success probability as well as on the number of triangles and vertices in the input graph. The space consumption for solving this problem is improved by Jowhari and Ghodsi [JG05] and further by Buriol et al. [BFL+06] where the dependency on the number of vertices is removed.

A paper of Buchsbaum et al. [BGW03] examines lower bounds for the problem of finding a pair of vertices that share a large common neighborhood. In particular, it is shown that any one-pass algorithm that is able to decide the existence of a vertex pair with a common neighborhood of size $1 < s < n$ requires $\Omega(n^2)$ bits of working memory in the worst case. This bound holds for deterministic as well as for randomized algorithms.

Ganguly and Saha [GS06] study the complexity to compute P_k, that is, the number of vertex pairs that are connected via a path of length k. It is shown that finding P_k in one pass over the input requires a memory of $\Omega(n^2)$ bits for any $k \geq 3$. A randomized algorithm with a memory consumption of $\mathcal{O}(\log n \cdot m(m-r)^{1/4})$ bits that estimates P_2 in a graph with r connected components is complemented with a lower bound of $\Omega(\sqrt{m})$ bits for that problem.

A formal motivation to extend the bound of $o(n)$ bits of memory when considering graph problems in the streaming context is given by Feigenbaum et al. [FKM+05a]: A large class of graph properties called balanced properties is identified whose determination in one pass requires $\Omega(n)$ space. Many basic properties as connectivity, bipartiteness, and the existence of a vertex with a certain degree fall into this class.

Muthukrishnan [Mut05] anticipates the leap over the $o(n)$ bit barrier when identifying a space restriction of $\mathcal{O}(n \cdot \text{polylog}\, n)$ bits as the sweet spot for streaming algorithms tackling graph problems. He suggests the corresponding semi-streaming model as defined in Chapter 2 and initiates the search for semi-streaming algorithms approaching different problems.

Two papers of Feigenbaum et al. [FKM+05b; FKM+05a] consider some basic problems in the semi-streaming model. Algorithms using one pass over the input are given to compute the connected components and a bipartition of a graph with a per-edge processing time of $T = \mathcal{O}(\alpha(n))$ and a minimum spanning forest with $T = \mathcal{O}(\log n)$. Here, $\alpha(n)$ denotes a natural inverse of Ackermann's function defined in Chapter 4. Moreover, [FKM+05b; FKM+05a] present algorithms testing a graph's k-vertex connectivity for $k \leq 4$ and its k-edge connectivity for any constant k using a single pass and a per-edge processing time increasing with n. Articulation points of a graph are shown to be obtainable in a single pass using $T = \mathcal{O}(n)$. In [Zel06] we show how to query the k-vertex connectivity of a graph with $T = \mathcal{O}(k^2 n)$ for every constant k.

The problem of finding a graph's matching in the semi-streaming model is first covered by Feigenbaum et al. [FKM+05b]. After observing that a maximal matching in an unweighted graph can trivially be found, an algorithm is given that $(\frac{3}{2} + \varepsilon)$-approximates a maximum matching in an unweighted bipartite graph for any $0 < \varepsilon < 3/2$ and whose number of passes depends on ε but is always at least three. For general unweighted graphs, a randomized multi-pass algorithm is given by McGregor [McG05] that $(1+\varepsilon)$-approximates a maximum matching for any $\varepsilon > 0$ using a number of passes larger than one depending on ε.

The same paper of McGregor [McG05] tweaks the semi-streaming algorithm that was given in [FKM+05b] approximating a maximum weighted matching in general graphs with a ratio of 6 in one pass to a ratio of 5.828. Furthermore, a multi-pass algorithm is presented that approximates a maximum weighted matching with a ratio of $2 + \varepsilon$ where the number of passes required over the input stream depends on ε and is larger than one.

It turnes out to be inherently difficult to compute distances between vertices in the streaming model. In particular, Feigenbaum et al. [FKM+05a] show that by using one pass and a memory of $O(n^{1+1/t})$ bits it is impossible to approximate the distance between two given vertices in an unweighted graph with a ratio better than t. If we let S_d be the vertices that have distance d to a specified vertex, this result can be broadened to multiple passes: In [FKM+05a] it is proven that the computation of S_d for $d \in \{1, \ldots, \lfloor t/2 \rfloor\}$ takes d passes if the space is restricted to $o(n^{1+1/t})$.

As a result, we get intractability of a breadth-first-search tree, even if it is of constant depth, for a one-pass semi-streaming algorithm. Moreover, a lower bound of $\Omega(\log n / \log \text{polylog}\, n)$ for the possible approximation ratio of distances in the semi-streaming model is obtained.

To estimate distances in the streaming model, there are approaches to compute an α-spanner of the input graph G, i.e, a subgraph of G in which the distance between each pair of vertices is at most their α-fold distance in G. The parameter α is called the stretch. Such spanners can be kept sparse to be storable within the memory of a streaming algorithm. During the postprocessing step, they allow to estimate the distance in question as well as the diameter and the girth.

A simple semi-streaming algorithm to compute a $\Theta(\log n / \log \log n)$-spanner of an unweighted graph using a per-edge processing time of $\mathcal{O}(n)$ is given by [FKM+05b]. In a series of papers [FKM+05a; Elk07; Bas08] this algorithm is improved via the introduction of randomization to reduce the per-edge processing time and to lower the stretch by constant factors.

We close this chapter by observing that there is work on related models that also cover graph problems in a streaming context but vary some aspects. In Bar-Yossef et al. [BYKS02] and Buriol et al. [BFL+06] incidence streams are studied where it is assumed that all edges incident to the same vertex appear subsequently in the stream. In [DFR06] and [DEMR07] the W-Stream model is considered that shapes an algorithm more powerful than a semi-streaming one: While reading the input stream, the algorithm outputs an intermediate stream that becomes the input stream for the next pass. The even more potent model of StrSort [ADRR04; Ruh03] is obtained if an intermediate stream of a W-Stream algorithm can be sorted according to some order on the data items before it is fed into the algorithm as the input stream for the next pass.

Chapter 4

Optimal Per-Edge Processing Times

4.1 Introduction

The semi-streaming model prohibits random access to the input graph and restricts the working memory. Despite this heavy restrictions compared to the traditional RAM model, there has been progress in designing semi-streaming algorithms that solve basic graph problems. In a paper by Feigenbaum et al. [FKM+05b], semi-streaming algorithms are developed for computing the connected components and a bipartition of a graph using a per-edge processing time of $T = \mathcal{O}(\alpha(n))$. In the same paper, the computation of a minimum spanning forest with $T = \mathcal{O}(\log n)$ is presented. For any constant k, there are approaches to determine the k-edge connectivity of a graph using $T = \mathcal{O}(n \log n)$ [FKM+05a] and the k-vertex connectivity using $T = \mathcal{O}(k^2 n)$ [Zel06].

In this chapter we present semi-streaming algorithms for all problems mentioned above that have constant and therefore optimal per-edge processing times. Our algorithms for k-vertex and k-edge connectivity are applicable as long as $k = \mathcal{O}(\text{polylog } n)$. Moreover, we can show that for each presented algorithm the computing time asymptotically equals the required time in the RAM model which therefore cannot convert the advantage of unlimited memory and random access into superior computing times for these problems.

The remaining part of this introduction gives the definitions required for the remaining chapter. We develop our semi-streaming algorithms in Section 4.2. Finally, in Section 4.3 we debate on how the obtained algorithms compete with the corresponding algorithms in the RAM model.

Every graph $G = (V, E)$ considered in this chapter is undirected and contains no loops but might have multiple edges. If G is a weighted graph, we presume every edge of G to be associated with a nonnegative weight and, regarding the memory constraint of the semi-streaming model, we assume every weight to be storable in $\mathcal{O}(\text{polylog } n)$ bits. Recall that we expect every graph to contain $\omega(n \cdot \text{polylog } n)$ edges since otherwise a per-edge processing time of $\mathcal{O}(1)$ can trivially be obtained by simply reading the whole graph into the working memory and examining it in the postprocessing step.

We define $\alpha(m, n)$ to be a natural inverse of Ackermann's function $A(\cdot, \cdot)$ as utilized by Tarjan [Tar83]: $\alpha(m, n) := \min\{i \geq 1 \mid A(i, \lfloor m/n \rfloor) > \log n\}$. We abbreviate $\alpha(n)$ to denote $\alpha(n, n)$.

A graph G is called *bipartite* if the vertices can be split in two parts, a *bipartition*, such that no edge runs between two vertices in the same part. The problem of finding a bipartition is to find two such parts or stating that there is no bipartition if the graph is not bipartite.

A *path* is a sequence of pairwise distinct vertices such that every two consecutive vertices in the sequence are adjacent. We name two vertices *connected* if there is a path between them. A graph G is connected if any pair of vertices in G is connected; a *connected component* of G is an induced subgraph C of G such that C is connected and maximal. A *spanning forest* of G is a subgraph of G without any cycles having the same connected components as G.

Given a positive integer k, a graph G is said to be k-*vertex connected* (k-*edge connected*) if the removal of any $k-1$ vertices (edges) leaves the graph connected. A subset S of the vertices (edges) of G we call an ℓ-*separator* (ℓ-*cut*) if $\ell = |S|$ and the graph obtained by removing S from G has more connected components than G. The *local vertex-connectivity* $\kappa(x,y;G)$ (*local edge-connectivity* $\lambda(x,y;G)$) denotes the number of internally vertex-disjoint (edge-disjoint) paths between x and y in G. By a classical result of Menger, see e.g. [Bol79], the local vertex- (edge-) connectivity between x and y equals the minimum number of vertices (edges) that must be removed to obtain x and y in different connected components.

For a weighted graph G, the *minimum spanning forest MSF* is a subgraph G' of G with minimum total edge weight sum that consists of the same connected components as G. If G is connected, we name G', which is then connected as well, a *minimum spanning tree MST* of G.

Given any graph property $\mathcal{P}$ and a graph G on the vertex set V. A *certificate* of G for $\mathcal{P}$ is a graph G' on V such that G has $\mathcal{P}$ if and only if G' has $\mathcal{P}$. A *strong certificate* of G for $\mathcal{P}$ is a graph G' on vertex set V such that for any graph H on V, $G \cup H$ has $\mathcal{P}$ if and only if $G' \cup H$ has $\mathcal{P}$. A certificate is said to be *sparse* if its number of edges is $\mathcal{O}(n \cdot \text{polylog}\, n)$. Note that a sparse certificate can be memorized within the restricted working memory of a semi-streaming algorithm.

4.2 Computing Certificates and Buffering Edges

To achieve our optimal per-edge processing times, we exploit the general method of sparsification as presented by Eppstein et al. [EGIN97]. Feigenbaum et al. [FKM+05a] pointed out how the results of [EGIN97] can be adopted for the semi-streaming model. Thus, they received the formerly best bounds on T for almost all problems considered in this chapter. We refine their method to obtain an improvement of their results. For a comparison of our new bounds with the previous ones see Table 4.1.

Due to the memory limitations of the semi-streaming model, it is not possible to memorize a whole graph which is too dense, that is, if $m = \omega(n \cdot \text{polylog}\, n)$. A way to determine graph properties without completely storing the graph is to find a sparse certificate C of the graph for the property in question. Consisting of $\mathcal{O}(n \cdot \text{polylog}\, n)$ edges, the certificate can be stored within the memory restriction and testing it answers the question for the original graph. The concept of certificates has been applied for the semi-streaming model in [FKM+05a] and [Zel06]. However, in [Zel06] every input edge initiates an update of the certificate which is time-consuming and avoids a faster per-edge processing.

4.2. Computing Certificates and Buffering Edges

Problem	Previous Best T	New T
Connected components	$\mathcal{O}(\alpha(n))$	$\mathcal{O}(1)$
Bipartition	$\mathcal{O}(\alpha(n))$	$\mathcal{O}(1)$
$\{2,3\}$-vertex connectivity	$\mathcal{O}(\alpha(n))$	$\mathcal{O}(1)$
4-vertex connectivity	$\mathcal{O}(\log n)$	$\mathcal{O}(1)$
k-vertex connectivity	$\mathcal{O}(k^2 n)$	$\mathcal{O}(1)$
$\{2,3\}$-edge connectivity	$\mathcal{O}(\alpha(n))$	$\mathcal{O}(1)$
4-edge connectivity	$\mathcal{O}(n\alpha(n))$	$\mathcal{O}(1)$
k-edge connectivity	$\mathcal{O}(n \cdot \log n)$	$\mathcal{O}(1)$
Minimum spanning forest	$\mathcal{O}(\log n)$	$\mathcal{O}(1)$

Table 4.1: Previously best per-edge processing times T compared to our new bounds. All previous bounds are due to Feigenbaum et al. [FKM+05a], apart from k-vertex connectivity which is a result of [Zel06]. For previous results, k is any constant, our results are applicable as long as $k = \mathcal{O}(\text{polylog}\, n)$. The term $\alpha(n)$ denotes an inverse of Ackermann's function.

To increase the manageable frequency of incoming edges, updating the certificate can be done not for every single edge but for a group of edges. While considering such a group of edges, the next incoming edges can be buffered to compose the group for the following update.

To permit this updating in groups of edges, the utilized certificate must be a strong certificate, an assumption that is not required in [Zel06]. As noted in [EGIN97], strong certificates obey two important attributes for any fixed graph property: First, they behave transitively, that is, if C is a strong certificate for G and C' is a strong certificate for C, then C' is a strong certificate for G. Second, if G' and H' are strong certificates of G and H respectively, then $G' \cup H'$ is a strong certificate of $G \cup H$.

The technique of group-wise updating used in [EGIN97] yielding fast dynamic algorithms has been transferred to the semi-streaming model by Feigenbaum et al. [FKM+05a]. The following theorem is a slightly enhanced version of their result augmented with space considerations. Note also that the following theorem is a straightforward extension of the theorem we proved in [Zel07]: Instead of certificates with $\mathcal{O}(n)$ edges, the following version is formulated with respect to certificates with $\mathcal{O}(n \cdot \text{polylog}\, n)$ edges.

Theorem 1 *Let G be a graph and let C be a sparse and strong certificate of G for a graph property $\mathcal{P}$. If C can be computed in space $\mathcal{O}(m)$ and time $f(n,m)$, then there is a one-pass semi-streaming algorithm building C of G with per-edge processing time of*

$$T = f(n, \mathcal{O}(n \cdot \text{polylog}\, n))/(n \cdot \text{polylog}\, n)$$

Proof. Define $r := n \cdot \text{polylog}\, n$. We denote the edges of the input stream as $e_1, e_2, \ldots, e_m$ and the subgraph of G containing the first i edges in the stream as G_i. We inductively assume that we computed a sparse and strong certificate C_{jr} of the graph G_{jr} for $1 \leq j < \lfloor m/r \rfloor$ using a per-edge processing time of $f(n, \mathcal{O}(r))/r$ per already processed edge. During the computation of C_{jr}, we buffered the next r edges $e_{jr+1}, e_{jr+2}, \ldots, e_{(j+1)r}$.

Due to the properties of strong certificates, $D = C_{jr} \cup \{e_{jr+1}, e_{jr+2}, \ldots, e_{(j+1)r}\}$ is a strong certificate for $G_{(j+1)r}$. Since C_{jr} is sparse, D consists of $\mathcal{O}(n \cdot \text{polylog}\, n)$ edges as well. The computation of $C_{(j+1)r}$ as a sparse and strong certificate of D can be realized in a space that linearly depends on the space needed to memorize the edges of D. Because D can be memorized within $\mathcal{O}(n \cdot \text{polylog}\, n)$ bits, the computation of $C_{(j+1)r}$ does not exceed the memory limitation of the semi-streaming model. By transitivity, $C_{(j+1)r}$ is a strong certificate of $G_{(j+1)r}$. A time of $f(n, \mathcal{O}(r))$ suffices to compute $C_{(j+1)r}$; hence, the input edges can arrive with a time delay of $f(n, \mathcal{O}(r))/r$ building the group of the next r edges to update the certificate after the computation of $C_{(j+1)r}$ is completed.

Finally, for $k = \lfloor m/r \rfloor$ the last group of edges $\{e_{kr+1}, e_{kr+2}, \ldots, e_m\}$ can simply be added to C_{kr} to obtain a sparse and strong certificate of the input graph G for the property $\mathcal{P}$. □

To obtain our semi-streaming algorithms with optimal per-edge processing times, all that remains to do is to present the required certificates and to show in which time and space bounds they can be computed. At first glance, it may seem surprising that Feigenbaum et al. [FKM+05a] using the same technique of updating certificates with groups of edges do not meet the bounds we present in this chapter. The reason is that they just observe results of Eppstein et al. [EGIN97] to be transferable to the semi-streaming model. However, in [EGIN97] dynamic graph algorithms are developed that require powerful abilities: The algorithm must be able to answer a query for the subgraph of already read edges at any time and it must handle edge deletions. In the semi-streaming model, the property is queried only at the end of the stream and there are no edge deletions. Thus, we can drop both requirements for faster per-edge processing times.

4.2.1 Connected Components

We use a spanning forest F of G as a certificate for connectivity. F is not only a strong certificate; it also has the same connected components as G. F can be computed by a depth-first search in time and space of $\mathcal{O}(n + m)$ and is sparse by definition. Using Theorem 1, we get a semi-streaming algorithm computing a spanning forest of G with per-edge processing time $T = \mathcal{O}(1)$. To identify the connected components of G in the postprocessing step, we can run a depth-first search on the final certificate in time $\mathcal{O}(n \cdot \text{polylog}\, n)$. The resulting computing time is $m \cdot T + \mathcal{O}(n \cdot \text{polylog}\, n) = \mathcal{O}(m)$ since we assume $m = \omega(n \cdot \text{polylog}\, n)$.

4.2.2 Bipartition

As a certificate for bipartiteness of G we use F^+, which is a spanning forest of G augmented with one more edge of G inducing an odd cycle if there is any. If no such cycle exists, F^+ is just a spanning forest. F^+ is sparse by definition and by [EGIN97] it is a strong certificate for bipartiteness of G. It can be computed by a depth-first search which alternately colors the visited vertices and is therefore able to find an odd cycle. To do so, a time and space of $\mathcal{O}(n+m)$ suffices, yielding a semi-streaming algorithm with $T = \mathcal{O}(1)$. On the final certificate, we can run again a depth-first search coloring the vertices alternately in time $\mathcal{O}(n \cdot \text{polylog}\, n)$ during the postprocessing step. That produces a bipartition of the vertices or identifies an odd cycle in G in a computing time of $\mathcal{O}(m)$.

4.2.3 k-Vertex Connectivity

For k-vertex connectivity, $k = \mathcal{O}(\text{polylog } n)$, we use as a certificate of G a subgraph C_k which is derived by an algorithm presented by Nagamochi and Ibaraki [NI92]. C_k can be computed in time and space of $\mathcal{O}(n+m)$, contains at most kn edges and is therefore sparse. Beyond it, as a main result of [NI92], C_k preserves the local vertex connectivity up to k for any pair of nodes in G:
$$\kappa(x, y; C_k) \geq \min\{\kappa(x, y; G), k\} \quad \forall x, y \in V \tag{4.1}$$
This quality of C_k leads to useful properties:

Lemma 2 *Every ℓ-separator S in C_k with $\ell < k$ is an ℓ-separator in G and its removal leaves the same connected components in both $C_k \setminus S$ and $G \setminus S$.*

Proof. In $C_k \setminus S$ we find two nonempty, disjoint connected components X and Y with vertices $x \in X$ and $y \in Y$. Assume that S is not an ℓ-separator in G; therefore, there exists a path Z from x to y in $G \setminus S$. Let x' be the last vertex on Z in X and y' the first one in Y. The part of Z between x' and y' we call Z'. In C_k we find at most ℓ vertex-disjoint paths between x' and y', all of them using vertices of S. In G these paths exist as well with the additional path Z' which is vertex-disjoint from the other paths by construction. Therefore, the local connectivity between x' and y' in G exceeds their local connectivity in C_k contradicting Property (4.1) of C_k.

Since $C_k \setminus S$ is a subgraph of $G \setminus S$, every connected component of $C_k \setminus S$ is included in one connected component of $G \setminus S$. Assume that W is a connected component in $G \setminus S$ which contains two vertices i and j within different connected components of $C_k \setminus S$, namely $I \ni i$ and $J \ni j$. As in the first part of this proof, we can find a path Z from i to j in W with x' being the last vertex in I and y' the first one in J on Z. We can deduce the same contradiction as above. □

So C_k is usable for our purposes:

Lemma 3 *C_k is a strong certificate for k-vertex connectivity of G.*

Proof. If $C_k \cup H$ is k-vertex connected, then $G \cup H$ including $C_k \cup H$ as a subgraph is k-vertex connected as well. Assume for the proof of the converse direction that $G \cup H$ is k-vertex connected and $C_k \cup H$ is not. Then $C_k \cup H$ contains an ℓ-separator S for some $\ell < k$. After the removal of S the remaining vertices of $C_k \cup H$ can be grouped into two nonempty sets A and B, such that no edge joins a vertex of A with a vertex of B. It is immediate that H does not contain any edges between A and B.

Clearly, removing S from C_k produces the same sets A and B, still with no edge joining them. The properties of C_k shown in Lemma 2 make sure that the removal of S from G leaves A and B without any joining edge, too. With H having no edges between A and B the graph $G \cup H$ cannot be k-vertex connected. □

Using Theorem 1 yields a semi-streaming algorithm computing a sparse and strong certificate of k-vertex connectivity with a per-edge processing time $T = \mathcal{O}(1)$. To test the final certificate for k-vertex connectivity in a postprocessing step, we can use an algorithm of Gabow [Gab06] on it that uses a space linear in the number of edges in the final certificate, hence, does not exceed the memory constraint of the semi-streaming model. That algorithm needs a time of $\mathcal{O}((n + \min\{k^{5/2}, kn^{3/4}\})kn)$ on general graphs. On our final certificate that results in a postprocessing time of $\mathcal{O}(kn^2)$ and in a computing time of $\mathcal{O}(m + kn^2) = \mathcal{O}(kn^2)$.

4.2.4 k-Edge Connectivity

We use the same C_k as utilized in Section 4.2.3 as our certificate. Nagamochi and Ibaraki [NI92] show that C_k reflects the local edge-connectivity of G in the following way:

$$\lambda(x, y; C_k) \geq \min\{\lambda(x, y; G), k\} \quad \forall x, y \in V \tag{4.2}$$

Therefore, Lemma 2 and Lemma 3 can be formulated and proven with respect to ℓ-cuts, $\ell < k$, and k-edge connectivity. Accordingly, we have a semi-streaming algorithm computing a strong and sparse certificate for k-edge connectivity using $T = \mathcal{O}(1)$. To determine k-edge connectivity of the final certificate, we can use an algorithm of Gabow [Gab95] using a space linear in the number of edges of the final certificate. It takes a time of $\mathcal{O}(m + k^2 n \log(n/k))$ on general graphs which is also the resulting computing time of our semi-streaming algorithm.

4.2.5 Minimum Spanning Forest

Let us first take a look at the algorithm we use as a subroutine for our semi-streaming algorithm computing an MSF of a given graph. We utilize the MST algorithm of Pettie and Ramachandran [PR02] which uses a space of $\mathcal{O}(m)$. A remark on how we use an algorithm computing an MST to obtain an MSF is given below. The algorithm of [PR02] uses a time of $\mathcal{O}(\mathcal{T}^*(m, n))$, where $\mathcal{T}^*(m, n)$ denotes the minimum number of edge-weight comparisons needed to find an MST of a graph with n vertices and m edges. The algorithm uses decision trees which are provably optimal but whose exact depth is unknown. Because of that, the exact running time of the algorithm is not known even though it is optimal.

The currently tightest time bound for the MST problem is given by algorithms due to Chazelle [Cha00] and Pettie [Pet99] that run in time $\mathcal{O}(m \cdot \alpha(m, n))$. Consequently, the optimal algorithm of Pettie and Ramachandran [PR02] inherits this running time; hence, we know that $\mathcal{T}^*(m, n) = \mathcal{O}(m \cdot \alpha(m, n))$. Based on the definition, $\alpha(m, n) = \mathcal{O}(1)$ if $m/n \geq \log n$. Therefore, on a sufficiently dense graph the algorithm of [PR02] computes an MST in time $\mathcal{O}(m)$.

Using this optimal algorithm as a subroutine, we can find a semi-streaming algorithm of per-edge processing time $T = \mathcal{O}(1)$ with the technique used in the proof of Theorem 1: Instead of computing a certificate of the input graph iteratively, we compute the MSF itself this way. By taking up the notation of the proof of Theorem 1, C_{jr} is the memorized MSF of the graph G_{jr} made up of the edges $e_1, e_2, \ldots, e_{jr}$ in the input stream. We merge the buffered next r edges with C_{jr} to build $D = C_{jr} \cup \{e_{jr+1}, e_{jr+2}, \ldots, e_{(j+1)r}\}$. For the number m_D of edges in D, we have $m_D \geq n \log n$ and therefore the optimal MST algorithm uses a time of $\mathcal{O}(m_D)$ to compute an MSF $C_{(j+1)r}$ of D. Since $m_D < 2r$, the computation of $C_{(j+1)r}$ takes a time of $\mathcal{O}(r)$. To fill the buffer of the next r edges in the meantime, the edges can arrive with a time delay of $\mathcal{O}(1)$.

It remains to show that what we compute in the described way is indeed an MSF of the input graph G. Every edge of G_{jr} that is not in C_{jr} is the heaviest edge on a cycle in G_{jr} and cannot be in an MSF of G. On the other hand C_{jr} does not contain any dispensable edges since it includes no cycles: The removal of any edge from C_{jr} produces two connected components in C_{jr} whose vertices form a common connected component in G_{jr}. Therefore, C_{jr} forms an MSF of G_{jr}, inductively showing that we really obtain an MSF of G in this manner.

Now we can state the computing time of our semi-streaming algorithm that finds an MSF of the input graph. This time is asymptotically optimal, even if the input graph does not contain $\omega(n \cdot \mathrm{polylog}\, n)$ edges.

If G has at most $r = n \log n$ edges, all edges are read into the working memory using a per-edge processing time $T = \mathcal{O}(1)$. Then the optimal algorithm of Pettie and Ramachandran [PR02] computes an MSF in time $\mathcal{O}(T^*(m,n))$, producing a computing time of $\mathcal{O}(T^*(m,n))$, since $\Omega(m)$ is a lower bound for $T^*(m,n)$.

If G has more than r edges, we iteratively compute an MSF. Note that, different from the described procedure in the proof of Theorem 1, the last group of buffered edges is not simply merged to $C_{\lfloor m/r \rfloor r}$ computed up to now. Instead, the MSF of the merged graph is calculated in the postprocessing step to obtain the final MSF which is also an MSF of the input graph. If the last group of edges does not comprise r edges, the last merged graph might have $m_f = o(n \log n)$ edges. Since $\mathcal{O}(T^*(m_f, n)) = \mathcal{O}(n \log n)$, for the computing time we get $m \cdot \mathcal{O}(1) + \mathcal{O}(n \log n) = \mathcal{O}(m)$ which again is $\mathcal{O}(T^*(m,n))$.

Let us give two minor remarks about the algorithm of Pettie and Ramachandran [PR02] we use. First, the algorithm of [PR02] assumes the edge weights to be distinct. We do not require that property since ties can be broken while reading the input edges in a way described in [EGIN97]. Second, the algorithm of [PR02] only works on connected graphs and therefore computes a MST instead of a more general MSF. However, before running that algorithm, we can use a depth-first search to identify the connected components which are then processed separately. Identifying the connected components takes a time of $\mathcal{O}(m) = \mathcal{O}(T^*(m,n))$, so the running time of our subroutine persists as well as the per-edge processing and the computing time of our semi-streaming algorithm.

4.3 Closure

In this section we compare the obtained semi-streaming algorithms to algorithms determining the same properties in the traditional RAM model allowing random access to all the edges of a graph and a working memory without any constraints.

First note that the presented semi-streaming algorithms have optimal per-edge processing times, that is, no semi-streaming algorithm exists allowing asymptotically shorter times: Every single edge must be considered to determine a solution for the problems considered in this chapter, so a time of $\Omega(1)$ per edge is a lower bound for these problems.

Let us now take a look at the presented semi-streaming algorithms testing k-vertex and k-edge connectivity. For k-vertex connectivity, the fastest algorithm in the RAM model to date is due to Gabow [Gab06] which runs in time $\mathcal{O}(kn^2)$ for k being $\mathcal{O}(\mathrm{polylog}\, n)$. This asymptotically equals our computing time, which is not surprising since we use Gabow's algorithm as our subroutine. We find the same situation when looking at k-edge connectivity. Our achieved computing time of $\mathcal{O}(m + k^2 n \log(n/k))$ is asymptotically as fast as the fastest algorithm in the RAM model due to Gabow [Gab95] which we use as a subroutine. So both of our connectivity algorithms have a computing time that is asymptotically the same as the fastest known corresponding algorithms in the RAM model.

It is possible that there are faster but still unknown algorithms in the RAM model for k-vertex and k-edge connectivity which cannot be utilized in the semi-streaming model because they consume too much space. However, this cannot be the case for the problems of finding connected components, a bipartition, and an MSF of a given graph. The presented semi-streaming algorithms have asymptotically the same computing time as the fastest possible algorithms in the RAM model. That can easily be seen for connected components and bipartition: We obtain in each case a computing time of $\mathcal{O}(m)$ which is trivially a lower bound for any algorithm in the RAM model solving these problems as we can assume that the input graph does not contain isolated vertices. For computing an MSF, we get a computing time of $\mathcal{O}(T^*(m,n))$, where $T^*(m,n)$ is the lower time bound for any RAM algorithm.

For the asymptotic time needed to determine a solution, there is no difference for k-edge and k-vertex connectivity between the currently fastest algorithms in the RAM model and the presented semi-streaming algorithms. Unless faster connectivity algorithms in the RAM model are developed, there is no demand for a random access to the edges and for a memory exceeding $\mathcal{O}(n \cdot \mathrm{polylog}\, n)$ bits. For computing the connected components, a bipartition, and an MSF, such a demand will never emerge since the presented semi-streaming algorithms have optimal computing times. Here, the RAM model cannot capitalize on its mighty potential of unlimited memory and random access to beat the computing times of the weaker semi-streaming model.

We close this section by indicating a tradeoff between memory consumption and computing time when calculating an MSF in the semi-streaming model. If the memory constraint of the semi-streaming algorithm is tightend from $\mathcal{O}(n \cdot \mathrm{polylog}\, n)$ to $\mathcal{O}(n \log^{2-\varepsilon} n)$ bits, $\varepsilon > 0$, only $s = \mathcal{O}(n \log^{1-\varepsilon} n)$ edges can be memorized. In this case we can store our certificate C_k and compute the k-vertex and k-edge connectivity only for $k = \mathcal{O}(\log^{1-\varepsilon} n)$. Moreover, the optimal MST algorithm we utilize as a subroutine takes a running time of $\mathcal{O}(T^*(s,n))$. Provided that $T^*(s,n) = \omega(s)$, we obtain a per-edge processing time of $\omega(1)$ and therefore a computing time of $\omega(m)$. Both bounds are significantly larger than the corresponding ones when $\mathcal{O}(n \cdot \mathrm{polylog}\, n)$ bits of memory are permitted. However, if it turns out that $T^*(m,n) = \mathcal{O}(m)$ for any m, it suffices to store $\Theta(n)$ edges to obtain the per-edge and the computing time both to be optimal.

Chapter 5

Weighted Matching

5.1 Introduction

Throughout the whole chapter, $G = (V, E)$ denotes a graph without multi-edges or loops. It is associated with a function $w : E \to \mathbb{R}^+$ that assigns a positive weight $w(e) > 0$ to each edge e. A *matching* in G is a subset M of the edges such that no two edges in M have a vertex in common. If we let $w(M) := \sum_{e \in M} w(e)$ be the weight of M, the *maximum weighted matching problem* is to find a matching in G that has maximum weight over all matchings in G. That problem is well studied in the traditional RAM model. There are exact solutions in polynomial time known, see [Sch03] for an overview. The fastest algorithm is due to Gabow [Gab90] and runs in time $\mathcal{O}(nm + n^2 \log n)$.

When processing massive graphs even the fastest exact algorithms computing a maximum weighted matching are too time-consuming. Examples where weighted matchings in massive graphs must be calculated are the refinement of nets used by finite element methods [MMH97] and the multilevel partitioning of graphs [MPD00].

To deal with such graphs, there has been effort in the traditional RAM model to find algorithms of a much shorter running time that compute solutions which are not necessarily optimal but have some guaranteed quality. Such an approximation algorithm is said to yield an α-approximation ratio if for every graph G the algorithm finds a matching M in G such that $w(M) \geq w(M^*)/\alpha$, where M^* is a matching of maximum weight in G.

A 2-approximation RAM algorithm computing a matching in time $\mathcal{O}(m)$ was given by Preis [Pre99]. The best known approximation ratio approachable in linear time is $3/2 + \varepsilon$ for an arbitrarily small but constant ε. This ratio is obtained by an algorithm of Drake and Hougardy [VH05] in time $\mathcal{O}(m \cdot (1/\varepsilon))$. An algorithm of Pettie and Sanders [PS04] gets the same ratio slightly faster using a time of $\mathcal{O}(m \cdot \log(1/\varepsilon))$.

There are approaches to the maximum weighted matching problem in the semi-streaming model. McGregor [McG05] presents an algorithm finding a $(2 + \varepsilon)$-approximative solution with a number of passes $P > 1$ depending on ε.

However, for some real-world applications even a second pass over the input stream is unfeasible. If observed phenomena are not stored and must be processed immediately as they happen, only a single pass over the input can occur. For the case of a one-pass semi-streaming

---

Shadow Matching(G, k)

1 $M := \emptyset$
2 **while** input stream is not empty
3   get next input edge $y_1 y_2$

4   Let $g_1 y_1, g_2 y_2$ be the edges of M sharing a vertex with $y_1 y_2$
5    $a_1 g_1 := \text{shadow-edge}(g_1 y_1, g_1)$
6    $a_2 g_2 := \text{shadow-edge}(g_2 y_2, g_2)$
7   Let $a_1 c_1$ be the edge of M covering vertex a_1
8   Let $a_2 c_2$ be the edge of M covering vertex a_2
9    $S := \{y_1 y_2, g_1 y_1, a_1 g_1, a_1 c_1, g_2 y_2, a_2 g_2, a_2 c_2\}$

10   Find an augmenting set $A \subseteq S$ that
      maximizes $r(A) := w(A) - k \cdot w(M(A))$
11   **if** $r(A) > 0$ **then**
12   store each edge in $M(A)$ as a shadow-edge of
        its adjacent edges in A
13     $M := (M \setminus M(A)) \cup A$
14   **endif**

15 **endwhile**

Figure 5.1: The algorithm Shadow Matching

algorithm, it is known that finding a maximum weighted matching is impossible in general graphs [FKM+05b]. A first one-pass semi-streaming algorithm approximating the maximum weighted matching problem with a ratio of 6 presented in [FKM+05b] was tweaked in [McG05] to a ratio of 5.828. Both algorithms use only a per-edge processing time of $\mathcal{O}(1)$.

In this chapter we present a semi-streaming algorithm that runs in one pass over the input, has a constant per-edge processing time, and approximates the maximum weighted matching problem on general graphs with a ratio of 5.585. Therefore, it surpasses the known semi-streaming algorithms computing a weighted matching in a single pass. In Section 5.2 we present our algorithm and its main ideas. While the proof of the approximation ratio is found in Section 5.3, we give some closing remarks in Section 5.4.

5.2 The Algorithm

By M^* we denote a matching of maximum weight in G and we let M in the following be a matching of G that is constructed by our algorithm. For a set of vertices W, we call $M(W)$ to be the set of edges in M covering a vertex in W. Correspondingly, for a set F of edges, we denote by $M(F)$ all edges in M that are adjacent to an edge in F. A set of edges in $E \setminus M$ such that every pair of edges in this set is not adjacent, we call an *augmenting set*. Throughout the whole chapter, k denotes a constant greater than 1.

5.2. THE ALGORITHM

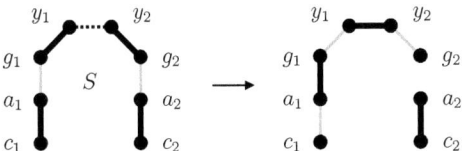

Figure 5.2: Example of an algorithm's step. Edges in M are shown in bold, shadow-edges appear in grey. y_1y_2 is the actual input edge shown dashed. The algorithm inserts the augmenting set $A = \{y_1y_2, a_1g_1\}$ into M. Therefore, the edges $M(A) = \{a_1c_1, g_1y_1, g_2y_2\}$ are removed from M, they become shadow-edges.

Our algorithm is given in Figure 5.1. Note at first that each edge in the algorithm is denoted by its endpoints, which is done for the sake of simpler considerations in the following on edges having common vertices. Every edge is well-defined by its endpoints since we assume the input graph G to contain no multi-edges.

The general idea of the algorithm is to keep a valid matching M of G at all times and to decide for each incoming edge y_1y_2 in the input stream if it is inserted into M. This is the case if the weight of y_1y_2 is big compared to the edges already in M sharing a vertex with y_1y_2 and that therefore must be removed from M to incorporate y_1y_2.

This idea so far has already been utilized by one-pass semi-streaming algorithms of Feigenbaum et al. [FKM+05b] and McGregor [McG05] seeking a matching in weighted graphs. The algorithm of [FKM+05b] is quite simple: Starting with an empty matching M, for every input edge e, it examines the at most two edges a, b already in M sharing a vertex with e. If $w(e) > k \cdot (w(a) + w(b))$ for $k = 2$, e replaces a and b in M. The resulting approximation ratio of 6 was improved in [McG05] to 5.828 by changing k to 1.707.

Even if the general approach of our algorithm is similar to both of the above algorithms, there are various important differences.

First, if the algorithms of Feigenbaum et al. [FKM+05b] and McGregor [McG05] remove an edge from the actual matching M, this is irrevocable. Our new algorithm, by contrast, stores some edges that have been in M in the past but were removed from it. To potentially reinsert them into M, the algorithm memorizes such edges under the name of shadow-edges. For an edge xy in M *shadow-edge*(xy, a), $a \in \{x, y\}$, denotes an edge that is stored by the algorithm and shares the vertex a with xy. Every edge xy in M has at most two shadow-edges assigned to it, at most one shadow-edge is assigned to the endpoint x and at most one is assigned to y.

A second main difference is the way of deciding if an edge e is inserted into M or not. In the algorithms of [FKM+05b] and [McG05], this decision is based only on the edges in M adjacent to e. Our algorithm takes edges in M as well as shadow-edges in the vicinity of e into account to decide the insertion of e.

Finally, the algorithms of [FKM+05b] and [McG05] are limited to the inclusion of the actual input edge into M. By reintegrating shadow-edges, our algorithm can insert up to three edges into M within a single step.

Let us take a closer look at the algorithm. As an example of a step of the algorithm, Figure 5.2

is given. But note that this picture shows only one possible configuration of the set S. Since non-matching edges in S may be adjacent, S may look different.

After reading the actual input edge y_1y_2, the algorithm tags all memorized edges in the vicinity of y_1y_2. This is done in lines 4-8. If an edge is not present, the corresponding tag denotes the null-edge, that is, the empty set of weight zero. Thus, if for example the endpoint y_2 of the input edge y_1y_2 is not covered by an edge in M, the identifier g_2y_2 denotes a null-edge as well as its shadow-edge a_2g_2 and the edge a_2c_2. All edges tagged so far are taken into consideration in the remaining part of the loop, they are subsumed to the set S in line 9.

In line 10 all augmenting sets of S are examined. Among these sets the algorithm selects A that maximizes $r(A)$. If $r(A) > 0$, the edges of A are taken into M and the edges in M sharing a vertex with edges in A are removed from M. We say A is *inserted* into M, this is done in line 13.

If an augmenting set A is inserted into M, this is always accompanied by storing the removed edges $M(A)$ as shadow-edges of edges in A in line 12. More precisely, every edge e in $M(A)$ is assigned as a shadow-edge to every edge in A that shares a vertex with e. If, as in the example given in Figure 5.2, $A = \{y_1y_2, a_1g_1\}$, the edge g_1y_1 that is adjacent to both edges in A is memorized under the name shadow-edge(y_1y_2, y_1) as well as under the name shadow-edge(a_1g_1, g_1). The edge a_1c_1 is stored as shadow-edge(a_1g_1, a_1), g_2y_2 as shadow-edge(y_1y_2, y_2). After inserting A, a_2g_2 is not memorized as a shadow-edge assigned to g_2y_2 any longer since g_2y_2 is not an edge in M after the step. That is indicated in Figure 5.2 by the disappearance of a_2g_2. However, if a_2g_2 was memorized as a shadow-edge of a_2c_2 before, this will also be the case after inserting A.

It is important to note that there is never an edge in M which is a shadow-edge at the same time: Edges only become shadow-edges if they are removed from M. An edge which is inserted into M is no shadow-edge anymore, since there is no edge in M it could be assigned to as a shadow-edge.

It is easy to see that our algorithm computes a valid matching of the input graph G.

Corollary 4 *Throughout the algorithm Shadow Matching(G, k), M forms a matching of G.*

Proof. This is true at the start of the algorithm since $M = \emptyset$. Whenever the algorithm modifies M in line 13, it inserts edges such that no pair of them is adjacent and removes all edges that are adjacent to the newly inserted ones. Therefore, M never includes two adjacent edges. □

Our algorithm may remind of algorithms due Drake and Hougardy [VH05] and due to Pettie and Sanders [PS04] approximating a maximum weighted matching in the RAM model. Starting from some actual matching M in a graph G, these algorithms look for short augmentations, that is, connected subgraphs of G having constant size in which edges in M and $E \setminus M$ can be exchanged to increase the weight of the actual matching.

From this point of view, our algorithm may suggest itself as it is reasonable to expect the notion of short augmentations to be profitable in the semi-streaming model as well. However, we are unable to use even the basic ideas of proving the approximation ratio in [VH05] and [PS04].

As well as the algorithms the proof concept relies on random access to the whole graph, a potential we cannot count on in the semi-streaming model.

Certainly, our algorithm can be considered as a natural extension of the semi-streaming algorithms by Feigenbaum et al. [FKM+05b] and McGregor [McG05] seeking a weighted matching. In fact, McGregor's algorithm [McG05], which is just a generalization of the one in [FKM+05b], is equivalent with a reduced version of our algorithm: If we omit lines 5-8 and line 12, that is, if we remove anything connected to shadow-edges, we get the algorithm described by McGregor. S reduces to $\{y_1y_2, g_1y_1, g_2y_2\}$ and the only augmenting set is y_1y_2 which depending on its weight replaces g_1y_1, g_2y_2 or not.

By the utilization of shadow-edges, the abilities of our algorithm go beyond the ones in [FKM+05b] and [McG05]. Therefore, we have to substantially enhance the proof techniques used therein to attest an improved approximation ratio of our algorithm. This is done in the next section.

5.3 Approximation Ratio

Consider an augmenting set A which covers the vertices $B \subseteq V$ and let $k > 1$ be some constant. We call $f_{A,k} : V \to \{x \in \mathbb{R} \mid 0 \leq x \leq 1\}$ an *allocation function* for A if the following holds:

- $\forall\, v \in V \setminus B : f_{A,k}(v) = 0$
- $\forall\, ab \in A : f_{A,k}(a) \cdot w(M(a)) + f_{A,k}(b) \cdot w(M(b)) \leq w(ab)/k$
- $\forall\, cd \in M(A) : f_{A,k}(c) + f_{A,k}(d) \geq 1$

If there exists such an allocation function $f_{A,k}$ for an augmenting set A, we call A to be *locally k-exceeding*. The intuition here is as follows: If for an augmenting set A we have $w(A) > k \cdot w(M(A))$, we could distribute the weight of the edges in $M(A)$ to the edges of A in such a way that every edge ab in A gets weight of at most $w(ab)/k$ distributed to it. If A satisfies the stronger condition of being locally k-exceeding, such a weight distribution can also be done with the additional property that the weight of an edge cd in $M(A)$ is distributed only to edges in A that are adjacent to cd.

Lemma 5 *Every augmenting set A inserted into M by the algorithm Shadow Matching(G, k) is locally k-exceeding.*

Proof. Since $A \subseteq \{y_1y_2, a_1g_1, a_2g_2\}$ and $r(A) > 0$, $1 \leq |A| \leq 3$. If A consists of only one edge, say y_1y_2, we have $w(g_1y_1) + w(g_2y_2) \leq w(y_1y_2)/k$ for the sum of the weights of the adjacent edges because of the satisfied condition in line 11. In that case the allocation function is $f_{A,k}(y_1) = f_{A,k}(y_2) = 1$ and A is locally k-exceeding.

Let A consist of two edges, say y_1y_2 and a_1g_1. Since every subset of A is an augmenting set as well which is not taken by the algorithm, it follows that $r(\{y_1y_2, a_1g_1\}) \geq r(\{y_1y_2\})$ and therefore

$$w(y_1y_2) + w(a_1g_1) - k \cdot (w(a_1c_1) + w(g_1y_1) + w(g_2y_2)) \geq w(y_1y_2) - k \cdot (w(g_1y_1) + w(g_2y_2))$$

Thus, $w(a_1g_1) \geq k \cdot w(a_1c_1)$ and because $r(\{y_1y_2, a_1g_1\}) \geq r(\{a_1g_1\})$, we can deduce similarly that $w(y_1y_2) \geq k \cdot w(g_2y_2)$. Hence, for the allocation function we can set $f_{A,k}(a_1) = f_{A,k}(y_2) = 1$. Since $r(A) > 0$, we can find appropriate values for $f_{A,k}(g_1)$ and $f_{A,k}(y_1)$, too.

For other configurations of A, it can be exploited correspondingly that $r(A) \geq r(A')$ for all subsets A' of A to show the existence of a allocation function for A in a similar way. □

Because of Corollary 4, we can take the final M of the algorithm as a valid solution for the weighted matching problem on the input graph G. It is immediate that the constant k is crucial for the weight of the computed solution and therefore determines the ratio up to which the algorithm approximates an optimal matching. The main part of this chapter is to prove the following theorem which we just state here and prove later.

Theorem 6 *Let M^* be an optimal matching in G and M be a matching constructed by Shadow Matching(G,k), $k > 1$. Then*

$$\frac{w(M^*)}{w(M)} \leq k + \frac{k}{k-1} + \frac{k^3 - k + 1}{k^2}$$

We call G_i the subgraph of G consisting of the first i input edges. Furthermore, M_i denotes the matching constructed by the algorithm after completing the while-loop for the ith input edge, that is, after all edges of G_i have been processed. An edge xy *prevents* an edge ab if ab is the ith input edge and $xy \in M_i$ shares an endpoint with ab; thus, ab is not taken into M by the algorithm. Note that an edge might be prevented by one or two edges. It is immediate that an input edge which is not taken into M by the algorithm is prevented by one or two edges.

An edge xy *replaces* an edge cd if xy and cd share a vertex, $cd \in M_{i-1}$, $xy \in M_i$, and therefore $cd \notin M_i$. An edge can replace up to two edges and can be replaced by up to two edges.

Consider $M^* = \{o_1, o_2, \ldots\}$ to be an optimal solution for the maximum weighted matching problem of G and let $M_i^* := M^* \cap G_i$. The edges $o_1, o_2, \ldots$ in M^* we call *optimal edges*. If $w(M_i) < w(M_i^*)$, some edges of M_i^* must be missing in M_i. There are two possible reasons for the absence of an edge $o_l \in M_i^*$ in M_i. First, there are edges in M_j, $j \leq i$, which prevented o_l. Second, $o_l \in M_j$, $j < i$, is replaced by one or two edges and not reinserted into M afterwards.

In any case we can make edges in $\bigcup_{h \leq i} M_h$ responsible for missing edges of M_i^* in M_i. We charge the weight of an optimal edge o_l to the edges in $\bigcup_{h \leq i} M_h$ that are responsible for the prevention or the removal of o_l. If such a charged edge in M is replaced by other edges, its charge is transferred to the replacing edges such that no charge is lost. After all we can sum up the charges of all edges in the final M_m to get $w(M^* \setminus M_m)$.

To bound $w(M_i^* \setminus M_i)$ as a multiple c of $w(M_i)$, it suffices to show that each edge $xy \in M_i$ carries a charge of at most $c \cdot w(xy)$. This technique has been carried out by Feigenbaum et al. [FKM+05b] and McGregor [McG05] to estimate the approximation ratios of their semi-streaming algorithms calculating a weighted matching.

We follow the same general idea but need a more sophisticated approach of managing the charge. This is due to two reasons. First, the algorithms of [FKM+05b] and [McG05] are limited to a simple replacement step which substitutes one or two edges by a single edge e.

That makes the charge transfer easy to follow since the charges of the substituted edges are transferred completely to e. Our algorithm, by contrast, is able to substitute several edges by groups of edges. The charge to be transferred must be distributed carefully to the replacing edges.

Second, in the algorithms of [FKM+05b] and [McG05] the decision whether to insert an input edge into M is determined only by the edges in M adjacent to the input edge. If an optimal edge o is not taken into M, the charge can simply be assigned to the at most two edges already in M that are adjacent to o. In our algorithm not only the edges in M that are adjacent to o specify if o is taken into M. In fact, several shadow-edges and other edges in M in the environment of o may codetermine if o is inserted into M. These ambient edges must be taken into account if charge has to be distributed for preventing o.

For our more sophisticated technique of managing the charges, we can think of every edge $xy \in M$ as being equipped with the values *charge of optimal edge* $coe(xy, x)$ and $coe(xy, y)$, one for every endpoint of xy. The value $coe(xy, x)$ is the charge that the edge in M^* which is covering the vertex x is charging to xy.

If an edge is removed from M, its charges are transferred to the one or two replacing edges. Therefore, in addition to its $coe(xy, x)$ and $coe(xy, y)$, every edge $xy \in M$ is equipped with a third value *aggregated charge* $ac(xy)$ which contains charges that xy takes over from edges replaced by xy. We define $T(xy) := coe(xy, x) + coe(xy, y) + ac(xy)$ as the sum of the charges of the edge xy.

The Shadow Matching algorithm examines the set S of at most seven edges for every input edge. If S for an actual input edge contains a C_5, i.e., a cycle on five edges, we refer to this situation as the C_5-*case*. By taking up the notation of the edges in S as defined by our algorithm, it is easy to see that the C_5-case can only occur if $a_1 = a_2$: Since $y_1 y_2$ is not a loop and $g_1 y_1$, $g_2 y_2 \in M$, the vertices in $\{g_1, y_1, y_2, g_2\}$ must be pairwise diverse. The only way of building a C_5 using the remaining edges is to equalize a_1 and a_2. The C_5-case is shown as shape (g) of Figure 5.3.

If an optimal edge is prevented by two edges, both of them must be charged. To this aim the weight of the prevented optimal edge is split into two partial weights that specify the exact amount of charge that each of the two preventing edges has to take. For such a partial weight, we can show the following.

Lemma 7 *Let ab and yz be in M_i and let the optimal edge o be prevented by ab and yz. Let ab share the vertex a with the optimal edge o and let bc be the shadow-edge(ab, b). Let cd be the edge in M_i that covers c and let no C_5-case occur when o is the actual input edge. Then we can split $w(o)$ into two partial weights such that for the partial weight p that ab has to take as a charge for preventing o one of the following conditions is satisfied:*

(I) $p \leq k \cdot w(ab) \leq k \cdot (w(ab) + w(cd)) - w(bc)$
 and ab, o, and bc do not form a triangle,

(II) $p \leq k \cdot (w(ab) + w(cd)) - w(bc) \leq k \cdot w(ab)$
 and ab, o, and bc do not form a triangle,

(III) $p \leq k \cdot w(ab)$
 and ab, o, and bc form a triangle.

At the same time, a corresponding statement holds for the partial weight $w(o) - p$ that yz has to take.

Proof. Again we pick up the notation of the edges in the set S as defined by the algorithm in Figure 5.1. We assume y_1y_2 to be an optimal edge prevented by other edges. To assert the statement of the lemma, we have to show that $w(y_1y_2)$ can be distributed to the preventing edges such that one of the cases (I)-(III) emerge. We consider the different possibilities that can occur if y_1y_2 is not inserted into the algorithm's matching M. To this aim we examine the potential shapes of S when y_1y_2 is the actual input edge that are shown in Figure 5.3. These potential shapes result from all possibilities how the non-matching edges in S may overlap. In particular, the non-matching edges of every possible S overlap in a way regarded by at least one shape of Figure 5.3.

We start with S being of shape (d) depicted in Figure 5.3. In this shape the non-matching edges $A = \{y_1y_2, a_1g_1, a_2g_2\}$ do not overlap at all; thus, A is an augmenting set. If none of the edges in A is taken into M by the algorithm, its condition in line 11 is violated for A and all its subsets. Therefore, the following inequalities hold:

$$w(y_1y_2) \leq k \cdot w(g_1y_1) + k \cdot w(g_2y_2) \tag{5.1}$$
$$w(y_1y_2) \leq k \cdot (w(g_1y_1) + w(a_1c_1)) - w(a_1g_1) + k \cdot w(g_2y_2) \tag{5.2}$$
$$w(y_1y_2) \leq k \cdot (w(g_2y_2) + w(a_2c_2)) - w(a_2g_2) + k \cdot w(g_1y_1) \tag{5.3}$$
$$w(y_1y_2) \leq k \cdot (w(g_1y_1) + w(a_1c_1)) - w(a_1g_1)$$
$$\qquad + k \cdot (w(g_2y_2) + w(a_2c_2)) - w(a_2g_2) \tag{5.4}$$

In this case we can split $w(y_1y_2)$ into two partial weights p_x, $x \in \{1,2\}$, and charge p_x to g_xy_x such that

$$p_x \leq k \cdot w(g_xy_x) \text{ and } p_x \leq k \cdot (w(g_xy_x) + w(a_xc_x)) - w(a_xg_x) \tag{5.5}$$

That results in case (I) or case (II) of the lemma, depending on which of the right-hand sides is smaller.

Since $w(y_1y_2) > 0$, we have $r(A) > r(\{a_1g_1, a_2g_2\})$. Because A is an augmenting set, it cannot be the case that both a_1g_1 and a_2g_2 are inserted into M without y_1y_2. Let one of the edges a_xg_x be taken into M, w.l.o.g. let this edge be a_1g_1. If y_1y_2 is not inserted into M, it is $r(\{a_1g_1\}) \geq r(\{a_1g_1, y_1y_2\})$ and $r(\{a_1g_1\}) \geq r(A)$. The resulting inequalities show that the whole weight of y_1y_2 can be charged to g_2y_2; thus, $p_2 = w(y_1y_2)$ satisfies condition (5.5).

Note that Figure 5.3 does not explicitly depict the case in which $a_1 = c_2$, $a_2 = c_1$ and S builds a C_6. However, this situation is covered by shape (d) anyway because the non-matching edges A still do not overlap at all. As a result, the considerations so far for shape (d) also apply if S is a C_6.

We close the considerations on A being an augmenting set with the special case in which $a_1g_1 = a_2g_2$ shown as shape (a) in Figure 5.3. Now S builds a C_4, $a_1c_1 = g_2y_2$, and $a_2c_2 = g_1y_1$. It is not possible that one of the edges $a_1g_1 = a_2g_2$ and y_1y_2 is inserted into M without the other. If no edge at all is inserted into M in this situation, we can deduce the inequalities (5.1)-(5.4).

It remains to consider the cases in which A is no longer an augmenting set, that is, the edges $\{y_1y_2, a_1g_1, a_2g_2\}$ overlap in some way. Note that $a_1 \neq y_1$ ($a_2 \neq y_2$, respectively) since

5.3. Approximation Ratio

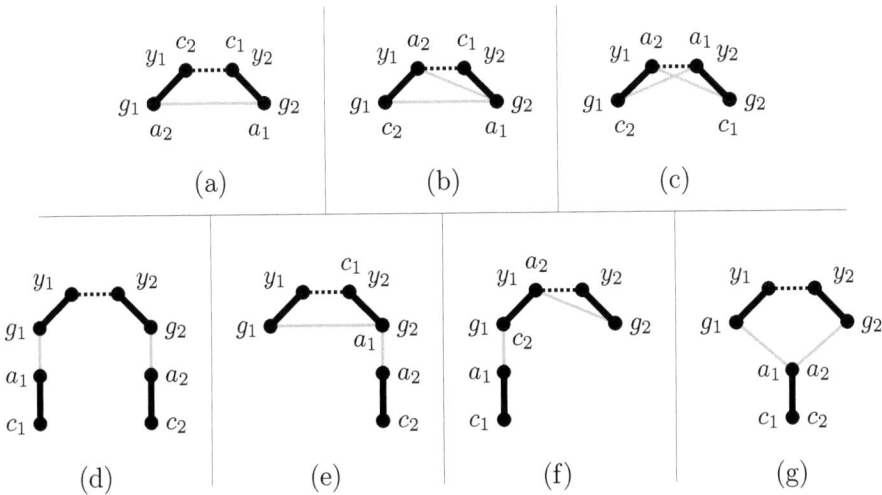

Figure 5.3: Illustration of all possible forms of S. Shapes (a)-(g) correspond to all possibilities (up to symmetry) how non-matching edges in S might overlap. The vertex labels correspond to the ones given by the Shadow Matching algorithm in Figure 5.1 when y_1y_2 shown dashed is the actual input edge. Edges in M appear bold, shadow-edges grey. Note that a vertex might get different labels as non-matching edges in S overlap.

otherwise $g_1y_1 = a_1g_1$ ($g_2y_2 = a_2g_2$) would be a shadow-edge and an edge in M at the same time which is not possible. We also have $a_1 \neq a_2$ since the C_5-case is excluded for this lemma.

Assume $a_1 = g_2$ and additionally $a_2 \neq y_1$ as shown by (e) in Figure 5.3. If no insertion at all takes place, the inequalities (5.1)-(5.4) can be deduced. Note that a_1g_1 cannot be inserted into M without the insertion of y_1y_2. If a_2g_2 is put into M without y_1y_2, we have $r(\{a_2g_2\}) \geq r(\{y_1y_2, a_2g_2\})$; therefore, $w(y_1y_2) \leq k \cdot w(g_1y_1)$. For the same reason, it is $r(\{a_2g_2\}) \geq r(\{y_1y_2, a_1g_1\})$; thus, $w(y_1y_2) \leq k \cdot (w(g_1y_1) + w(a_2g_2)) - w(a_1g_1)$. Now the whole weight $w(y_1y_2)$ can be charged to g_1y_1 satisfying (I) or (II) of the lemma. That is because a_2g_2 now plays the role of a_1c_1 as it covers a_1 as a matching edge.

Let second $a_2 = y_1$ and still $a_1 = g_2$, see shape (b) in Figure 5.3. If no insertion into M occurs, we can deduce (5.1) and (5.2). We can charge g_2y_2 with $p_2 = k \cdot w(g_2y_2)$ satisfying (III) of the lemma since g_2y_2, the input edge y_1y_2, and the shadow-edge a_2g_2 form a triangle. The remaining charge $p_1 = w(y_1y_2) - p_2$ can be taken by g_1y_1 meeting condition (5.5) because of (5.1) and (5.2). If for this shape of S an insertion without y_1y_2 happens, only a_2g_2 can be inserted. In this case it follows $w(y_1y_2) \leq w(a_2g_2)$ and $w(y_1y_2)$ can be completely charged to a_2g_2 which is in M now and builds a triangle with its shadow-edge g_2y_2 and the input edge y_1y_2. Thus, (III) is achieved.

We keep $a_2 = y_1$ but let $a_1 \neq g_2$ and $a_1 \neq y_2$ as shown by (f) in Figure 5.3. If no insertion occurs, we can again charge $k \cdot w(g_2y_2)$ to g_2y_2 meeting (III) and the remaining charge to g_1y_1. Since we can conclude (5.1) and (5.2), this remaining charge satisfies (I) or (II). If only a_1g_1 is put into M, we know that $w(y_1y_2) \leq k \cdot w(g_2y_2)$ and g_2y_2 can take the whole weight of y_1y_2 achieving (III). If a_2g_2 is inserted into M, it must be $w(y_1y_2) \leq w(a_2g_2)$ and a_2g_2 can be charged with $w(y_1y_2)$ meeting (III).

Let finally $a_1 = y_2$ and $a_2 = y_1$ as presented by (c) of Figure 5.3. If no edge is put into M, we know that (5.1) holds and $w(y_1y_2)$ can be split into two parts that are charged to g_1y_1 and g_2y_2, each satisfying (III). If one of a_1g_1 and a_2g_2 is inserted into M, the other one is inserted, too. In this case $w(y_1y_2) \leq w(a_1g_1) + w(a_2g_2)$ and we can split $w(y_1y_2)$ into two parts that meet (III) when charged to a_1g_1 and a_2g_2. □

During the proof of the following lemma, we will explicitly show how the edges in M take over charge from the edges they replace and prevent such that particular properties hold.

Lemma 8 *Let M_i be the solution of the algorithm Shadow Matching(G, k), $k > 1$, after reading G_i for $1 \leq i \leq m$. To every edge xy in M_i we can assign three values $coe(xy, x)$, $coe(xy, y)$, and $ac(xy)$, with $T(xy)$ being their sum, such that:*

a) $\sum_{xy \in M_i} T(xy) \geq w(M_i^* \setminus M_i)$

b) $\forall\ xy \in M_i$: $coe(xy, x) \leq k \cdot w(xy)$ and
$coe(xy, y) \leq k \cdot w(xy)$

c) $\forall\ xy \in M_i$: $ac(xy) \leq \frac{k}{k-1} \cdot w(xy)$

Proof. We prove the lemma by induction over the edges inserted into M. For the initial step of our induction, note that the properties of the lemma hold right after the first edge was inserted into M. For the inductive step, let y_1y_2 be an edge that is taken into M_i when the ith input edge is processed by the algorithm and let the statements of the lemma hold for M_{i-1}. Note that not necessarily y_1y_2 is the ith input edge, it is just part of the augmenting set inserted into M_i when the ith input edge is under examination by the algorithm.

We have to consider two things: First, we have to point out how the charges of the edges in M_{i-1} that y_1y_2 replaces are carried over to y_1y_2 to preserve the properties of the lemma. Second, we have to regard the at most two optimal edges that possibly come after y_1y_2 and share a vertex with y_1y_2. If y_1y_2 prevents one or both of these edges, we have to show how y_1y_2 is charged by them without violating the lemma.

As an edge that is inserted into M, y_1y_2 is part of an augmenting set A. Due to Lemma 5, A is locally k-exceeding; hence, there exists an allocation function $f_{A,k}$ at the moment y_1y_2 is inserted into M.

In the following let $x \in \{1, 2\}$. The edge y_1y_2 takes over charges from g_xy_x, that is, the edges it replaces. According to the allocation function $f_{A,k}$, y_1y_2 takes over a $f_{A,k}(y_x)$-fraction of the charges of g_xy_x. In fact, y_1y_2 builds its ac as follows:

$$ac(y_1y_2) := f_{A,k}(y_1) \cdot (coe(g_1y_1, g_1) + ac(g_1y_1)) + f_{A,k}(y_2) \cdot (coe(g_2y_2, g_2) + ac(g_2y_2))$$

By the induction hypothesis,

$$coe(g_xy_x, g_x) \leq k \cdot w(g_xy_x) \quad \text{and} \quad ac(g_xy_x) \leq w(g_xy_x) \cdot k/(k-1)$$

5.3. APPROXIMATION RATIO

Due to the definition of an allocation function,

$$f_{A,k}(y_1) \cdot w(g_1 y_1) + f_{A,k}(y_2) \cdot w(g_2 y_2) \leq w(y_1 y_2)/k$$

Thus, $ac(y_1 y_2) \leq w(y_1 y_2) \cdot k/(k-1)$ satisfies property c).
Furthermore, $y_1 y_2$ takes over charge from $coe(g_x y_x, y_x)$, again a $f_{A,k}(y_x)$-fraction of it:

$$coe(y_1 y_2, y_x) := f_{A,k}(y_x) \cdot coe(g_x y_x, y_x)$$

If $g_x y_x$ is an optimal edge, $coe(g_x y_x, y_x) = 0$ and $y_1 y_2$ instead takes over a $f_{A,k}(y_x)$-fraction of $w(g_x y_x)$ as its $coe(y_1 y_2, y_x)$ for replacing the optimal edge $g_x y_x$.

Note that whenever $f_{A,k}(y_x) < 1$, $y_1 y_2$ does not take over all the charge of $g_x y_x$. However, the definition of the allocation function together with Lemma 5 makes sure that we can deduce $f_{A,k}(g_x) \geq 1 - f_{A,k}(y_x)$ and that another edge in A covering g_x takes over the remaining charge of $g_x y_x$. That way no charge can get lost and property a) holds.

Let us check the validity of property b). Right after $y_1 y_2$ was inserted into M and took over the charges as described from $g_x y_x$, it holds that

$$coe(y_1 y_2, y_x) \leq f_{A,k}(y_x) \cdot k \cdot w(g_x y_x) \leq k \cdot w(y_1 y_2)/k$$

However, that does not suffice to show the validity of property b). In fact, there might be an optimal edge $o_x y_x$ coming after $y_1 y_2$ in the input stream covering y_x. In that case $coe(y_1 y_2, y_x) = 0$ up to this moment since there cannot be another optimal edge besides $o_x y_x$ covering y_x. If $o_x y_x$ is not inserted into M, that is, if $y_1 y_2$ prevents $o_x y_x$, $y_1 y_2$ must be charged.

If no C_5-case occurs when $o_x y_x$ is the actual input edge, we can apply Lemma 7. It covers all possible ways in which an edge in M can be charged for preventing an optimal edge. In all three possibilities (I)-(III), the charge that $y_1 y_2$ has to take as $coe(y_1 y_2, y_x)$ for preventing $o_x y_x$ is at most $k \cdot w(y_1 y_2)$ and therefore satisfies property b).

Let otherwise a C_5-case emerge when $o_x y_x$ is the actual input edge. However, the sum of the weights of the edges preventing $o_x y_x$ must be at least $w(o_x y_x)/k$. Hence, we can distribute $w(o_x y_x)$ as a charge to the preventing edges such that every preventing edge is charged by at most its k-fold weight. Again, $coe(y_1 y_2, y_x)$ does not exceed $k \cdot w(y_1 y_2)$ and property b) holds. □

From Lemma 8 we can only deduce that each edge in the algorithm's solution might carry a charge of at most the $2k + k/(k-1)$-fold of its own weight. This approximation ratio is precisely the one that is achieved by the algorithm of McGregor [McG05]. As a matter of fact, we can use our developed framework of the different types of charges per edge, their creation and transfer to replacing edges to reprove the approximation ratio obtained in [McG05]. To this aim no shadow-edges must be taken into account, the set S of our algorithm is reduced to $\{y_1 y_2, g_1 y_1, g_2 y_2\}$. That drastically simplifies Lemma 7 since there are no adjacent non-matching edges in S. Lemma 8 can be proven without considering the C_5-case and asserts the approximation ratio.

To surpass the ratio of McGregor's algorithm, we can show that the different types of the charges on every edge in M do not reach their maximum values described in Lemma 8 simultaneously. The specific statement is formulated by the next lemma and its proof uses shadow-edges as an essential part.

Lemma 9 *Let M_i be the solution of the algorithm Shadow Matching(G, k), $k > 1$, after reading G_i for $1 \leq i \leq m$. Additionally to a)-c) of Lemma 8, it holds that*

d) $\forall \ xy \in M_i: \ T(xy) \leq \left(k + \frac{k}{k-1} + \frac{k^3-k+1}{k^2}\right) \cdot w(xy)$

Proof. Again we prove the lemma by induction on the edges inserted into M. Obviously, the lemma holds right after the insertion of the first edge into M. Let the statement of the lemma be true for M_{i-1} and let $y_1 y_2 \notin M_{i-1}$ be taken into M_i via an augmenting set A.

Consider the moment immediately after $y_1 y_2$ was inserted into M_i and took over the charges from the replaced edges as described in the proof of Lemma 8. It is $ac(y_1 y_2) \leq w(y_1 y_2) \cdot k/(k-1)$ by c) of Lemma 8 and $coe(y_1 y_2, y_x) \leq w(y_1 y_2)$ for $x \in \{1, 2\}$ as carried out in the proof of Lemma 8. Therefore, $T(y_1 y_2)$ as their sum meets property d).

We now have to concern optimal edges $o_x y_x$ that are prevented by $y_1 y_2$ and therefore cause charge p_x at $coe(y_1 y_2, y_x)$. We show how to handle this charge such that $T(y_1 y_2)$ can be bounded as claimed.

We postpone to the end of the proof the situation in which an edge in M^* as the actual input edge causes a C_5-case and is prevented. In particular, we assume that none of the optimal edges $o_x y_x$ prevented by $y_1 y_2$ causes a C_5-case.

Let $g_1 y_1$ denote the shadow-edge$(y_1 y_2, y_1)$ and $g_2 y_2$ denote the shadow-edge$(y_1 y_2, y_2)$. Let p_x be the charge that $y_1 y_2$ has to take into its $coe(y_1 y_2, y_x)$ for preventing $o_x y_x$. The charge p_x satisfies one of the cases (I)-(III) of Lemma 7.

As described, $ac(y_1 y_2)$ is composed of four values, in particular, fractions of $ac(g_x y_x)$ and $coe(g_x y_y, g_x)$. The value of the part of $ac(g_x y_x)$ that is taken over into $ac(y_1 y_2)$ we call $ac(g_x y_x) \frown ac(y_1 y_2)$, correspondingly we call $coe(g_x y_x, g_x) \frown ac(y_1 y_2)$ the value of the part of $coe(g_x y_x, g_x)$ that is taken over by $ac(y_1 y_2)$. Using this notation we can separate $T(y_1 y_2)$ into two halves as follows:

$$T(y_1 y_2) = \Big(coe(y_1 y_2, y_2) + ac(g_1 y_1) \frown ac(y_1 y_2) + coe(g_1 y_1, g_1) \frown ac(y_1 y_2) \Big)$$
$$+ \Big(coe(y_1 y_2, y_1) + ac(g_2 y_2) \frown ac(y_1 y_2) + coe(g_2 y_2, g_2) \frown ac(y_1 y_2) \Big)$$

Let us call the upper half $H1$ and the lower one $H2$. We will estimate $H2$ in the following according to the three possible cases for p_1 and show that

$$H2 \leq \left(k + \frac{1}{k-1} + \frac{1}{k}\right) \cdot w(g_2 y_2) \cdot f_{A,k}(y_2) + k \cdot w(y_1 y_2) \qquad (*)$$

We will see later that it suffices to show that if neither $H2$ violates inequality (*) nor $H1$ violates a corresponding inequality, property d) holds for $y_1 y_2$.

Case 1
Charge p_1 coming from $o_1 y_1$ satisfies (I)
Let $g_2 z_2$ be an edge in M covering g_2. We can bound p_1 due to property (I):

$$p_1 \leq k \cdot w(y_1 y_2) \leq k \cdot (w(y_1 y_2) + w(g_2 z_2)) - w(g_2 y_2) \qquad (5.6)$$

5.3. Approximation Ratio

Let $uw \in M$ and let $uv := \text{shadow-edge}(uw, u)$. The edge uw was inserted into M as part of the augmenting set A'. We call uv *overloaded* if $coe(uv, v) \curvearrowright ac(uw) > w(uv) \cdot f_{A',k}(u)$. In our case, the shadow-edge g_2y_2 of y_1y_2 is overloaded if $coe(g_2y_2, g_2) \curvearrowright ac(y_1y_2) > w(g_2y_2) \cdot f_{A,k}(y_2)$. For uv we say that uv *fingers* v if uv covers v and v is not the vertex that uv shares with the edge uw it is assigned to. For example, the shadow-edge g_2y_2, which is assigned to y_1y_2, fingers g_2 but not y_2. A shadow-edge uv is *prepared* if for the edge uw in M that uv is assigned to $coe(uw, w) = 0$. So in the present example, g_2y_2 is prepared if $coe(y_1y_2, y_1) = 0$.

If $p_1 \leq k \cdot w(y_1y_2) - f_{A,k}(y_2) \cdot w(g_2y_2)$ or if g_2y_2 is not overloaded, we can simply add p_1 to $coe(y_1y_2, y_1)$ and $H2$ satisfies (*). Otherwise we do a *charge transfer* as follows: We reduce $coe(g_2y_2, g_2) \curvearrowright ac(y_1y_2)$ to $r := \max\{coe(g_2y_2, g_2) \curvearrowright ac(y_1y_2) - (k-1) \cdot w(g_2z_2), 0\}$ and add a value of $coe(g_2y_2, g_2) \curvearrowright ac(y_1y_2) - r$ to $coe(g_2z_2, g_2)$; thus, no charge is lost.

Of course, it is required to show that increasing $coe(g_2z_2, g_2)$ in this way does not violate properties b) of Lemma 8 and d) for g_2z_2: We know that $coe(g_2z_2, z_2) \leq k \cdot w(g_2z_2)$ and $ac(g_2z_2) \leq w(g_2z_2) \cdot k/(k-1)$. If before the charge transfer $coe(g_2z_2, g_2) = 0$, after the transfer property b) still holds and $T(g_2z_2)$ cannot exceed $(k + k/(k-1) + (k^3 - k + 1)/(k^2)) \cdot w(g_2z_2)$.

If otherwise $coe(g_2z_2, g_2) > 0$ before the charge transfer, we need a few considerations. In fact, we will use the following:

Claim:
For every vertex v and at any time of the algorithm, at most one shadow-edge fingers v, is overloaded, and prepared at the same time.

Proof of Claim: Assume that uv is the first shadow-edge created by the algorithm that is fingering v, is overloaded, and prepared. This can only be the case if uv in M gets replaced by uw and possibly vs. Right after the replacement, it must be $coe(vs, v) \leq w(vs)$. As long as no charge of $coe(uv, v) \curvearrowright ac(uw)$ is transferred to an edge in M covering v, for every edge vq in M covering v, $coe(vq, v) \leq w(vq)$. Such an edge vq cannot be turned into a shadow-edge fingering v and being overloaded. A second overloaded shadow-edge fingering v can only be created by replacing an edge vr with $coe(vr, v) > w(vr)$. That can only occur if uw transfers charge to vr. However, uw only transfers charge to vr if it prevents an optimal edge covering w. Afterwards, $coe(uw, w) > 0$ and uv is not prepared anymore. This shows that a prepared and overloaded shadow-edge fingering v can only be created if the at most one previously prepared and overloaded shadow-edge fingering v lost its status as being prepared. That proves the claim.

Now we can come back to the case $coe(g_2z_2, g_2) > 0$. We can assume that g_2z_2 as part of the augmenting set A' replaced the edges d_2g_2 and t_2z_2. The edge g_2z_2 took over a $f_{A',k}(g_2)$-fraction of the charges from d_2g_2. Since $coe(d_2g_2, g_2) \leq k \cdot w(d_2g_2)$ before the replacement of d_2g_2, we can deduce $coe(g_2z_2, g_2) \leq f_{A',k}(g_2) \cdot k \cdot w(d_2g_2)$ after the replacement. By the definition of an allocation function, $coe(g_2z_2, g_2) \leq w(g_2z_2) - f_{A',k}(z_2) \cdot k \cdot w(t_2z_2)$. After our charge transfer of weight at most $(k-1) \cdot w(g_2z_2)$ from $coe(g_2y_2, g_2) \curvearrowright ac(y_1y_2)$ to $coe(g_2z_2, g_2)$, it holds that $coe(g_2z_2, g_2) \leq k \cdot (w(g_2z_2) - f_{A',k}(z_2) \cdot w(t_2z_2))$. Therefore, $coe(g_2z_2, g_2)$ still satisfies b) of Lemma 8. Furthermore, we have

$$coe(g_2z_2, g_2) + coe(t_2z_2, t_2) \curvearrowright ac(g_2z_2) + ac(t_2z_2) \curvearrowright ac(g_2z_2)$$
$$\leq k \cdot w(g_2z_2) + f_{A',k}(z_2) \cdot w(t_2z_2) \cdot \left(\frac{k}{k-1}\right)$$

after the transfer. That shows that an inequality corresponding to (*) holds for g_2z_2 which certifies property d) for g_2z_2.

At this moment the above considerations are important: We know that no shadow-edge besides g_2y_2 that is fingering g_2 is prepared and overloaded. Thus, beside to the described one from $ac(y_1y_2)$, no further charge transfer to $coe(g_2z_2, g_2)$ can occur that might violate b) of Lemma 8 or d).

After transferring a part of $coe(g_2y_2, g_2) \curvearrowright ac(y_1y_2)$ as described above, we can deduce $coe(g_2y_2, g_2) \curvearrowright ac(y_1y_2) \leq \max\{k \cdot f_{A,k}(y_2) \cdot w(g_2y_2) - (k-1) \cdot w(g_2z_2), 0\}$. We add p_1 to $coe(y_1y_2, y_1)$ and can evaluate $H2$: Because of (5.6) we have $coe(y_1y_2, y_1) = p_1 \leq k \cdot w(y_1y_2)$ and by the induction hypothesis it holds that $ac(g_2y_2) \curvearrowright ac(y_1y_2) \leq f_{A,k}(y_2) \cdot w(g_2y_2) \cdot k/(k-1)$. Since $w(g_2z_2) \geq w(g_2y_2)/k$ due to (5.6), we can estimate $H2$ as being bounded as in inequality (*).

Case 2
Charge p_1 coming from o_1y_1 satisfies (II)
With g_2z_2 again being the edge in M covering g_2, we have in this case

$$p_1 \leq k \cdot (w(y_1y_2) + w(g_2z_2)) - w(g_2y_2) \leq k \cdot w(y_1y_2) \tag{5.7}$$

This case is very similar to the previous one. The only difference is that $w(g_2z_2) \leq w(g_2y_2)/k$ and we use $p_1 \leq k \cdot (w(y_1y_2) + w(g_2z_2)) - w(g_2y_2)$, both because of (5.7). All other considerations remain the same and that results in the very same estimation for $H2$.

Case 3
Charge p_1 coming from o_1y_1 satisfies (III)
In this case $o_1 = g_2$ since the input edge o_1y_1, the edge $y_1y_2 \in M$, and the shadow-edge g_2y_2 form a triangle. Since g_2y_1 is an optimal edge, before its arrival it is $coe(g_2y_2, g_2) \curvearrowright ac(y_1y_2) = 0$. So y_1y_2 can take a charge of $p_1 \leq k \cdot w(y_1y_2)$ into its $coe(y_1y_2, y_1)$ and $H2$ satisfies (*).

In each of the three cases, we can handle the charge p_1 such that $H2$ satisfies (*). By a symmetric argumentation, $H1$ satisfies a corresponding inequality. We can use the property of an allocation function, i.e., $f_{A,k}(y_1) \cdot w(g_1y_1) + f_{A,k}(y_2) \cdot w(g_2y_2) \leq w(y_1y_2)/k$, to get validity of property d) due to

$$T(y_1y_2) = H1 + H2 \leq \left(k + \frac{k}{k-1} + \frac{k^3 - k + 1}{k^2}\right) \cdot w(y_1y_2)$$

The C_5-Case
It remains to consider the postponed situation in which a C_5-case occurs when an optimal edge is prevented. Let $y_1y_2 \in M^*$ be the actual input edge that causes a C_5-case. Let g_1y_1, g_2y_2 be the edges in M sharing a vertex with y_1y_2 and let a_1g_1, a_2g_2 be their shadow edges at the opposite of y_1y_2. It must be $a_1 = a_2$ to close the C_5; the edge in M that covers that vertex we call a_1c_1. The situation is shown as shape (g) of Figure 5.3.

Consider at first the case that one of the edges a_1g_1, a_2g_2 is taken into M without y_1y_2; w.l.o.g. let this edge be a_1g_1. In this case it must be $r(\{a_1g_1\}) \geq r(\{a_1g_1, y_1y_2\})$; therefore, it must be $w(y_1y_2) \leq k \cdot w(g_2y_2)$ and because of $r(\{a_1g_1\}) \geq r(\{a_2g_2, y_1y_2\})$, we can

5.3. Approximation Ratio

deduce $w(y_1y_2) \leq k \cdot (w(g_2y_2) + w(a_1g_1)) - w(a_2g_2)$. Hence, $w(y_1y_2)$ can be charged completely to g_2y_2 to satisfy two inequalities corresponding to (5.5). Thus, the charge that g_2y_2 has to take meets (I) or (II) of Lemma 7 which was covered by Case 1 and Case 2 above.

In the last possibility no augmenting set is inserted into M at all. At the moment g_1y_1 was inserted into M, it took over a $f_{A',k}(g_1)$-fraction of the charges from a_1g_1 when replacing it. Correspondingly, g_2y_2 took over a $f_{A'',k}(g_2)$-fraction of the charges from a_2g_2 when it was taken into M.

Let w.l.o.g. $f_{A',k}(g_1) \cdot w(a_1g_1) \geq f_{A'',k}(g_2) \cdot w(a_2g_2)$. Prior to the arrival of y_1y_2, it is $coe(g_1y_1, y_1) = coe(g_2y_2, y_2) = 0$; thus, a_1g_1 and a_2g_2 are both prepared and fingering a_1. In the case that $coe(a_2g_2, a_2) \curvearrowright ac(g_2y_2) = f_{A'',k}(g_2) \cdot w(a_2g_2) + X$ for $X > 0$, a_2g_2 is overloaded. By the proved claim under Case 1, a_1g_1 cannot be overloaded as well; therefore, we have $coe(a_1g_1, a_1) \curvearrowright ac(g_1y_1) \leq f_{A',k}(g_1) \cdot w(a_1g_1)$. X cannot be greater than $(k-1) \cdot f_{A',k}(g_2) \cdot w(a_2g_2)$; as a result, we can transfer a charge of this weight X from $coe(a_2g_2, a_2) \curvearrowright ac(g_2y_2)$ to $coe(a_1g_1, a_1) \curvearrowright ac(g_1y_1)$. Since a_1g_1 is not overloaded before this transfer, c) of Lemma 8 still holds for $ac(g_1y_1)$. The edge a_1g_1 might get overloaded while a_2g_2 is not overloaded anymore.

After this transfer of charge, or if no transfer was necessary at all because $X \leq 0$, we have $coe(a_2g_2, a_2) \curvearrowright ac(g_2y_2) \leq f_{A'',k}(g_2) \cdot w(a_2g_2)$. Therefore, $coe(g_2y_2, y_2)$ can take a charge of $k \cdot w(g_2y_2)$ without violating the statement of the lemma since in that case $coe(g_2y_2, y_2)$ as well as $coe(a_2g_2, a_2) \curvearrowright ac(g_2y_2)$ and $ac(a_2g_2) \curvearrowright ac(g_2y_2)$ still satisfy an inequality corresponding to (*). If no augmenting set is inserted into M, it follows that

$$w(y_1y_2) \leq \min\left\{k \cdot (w(g_1y_1) + w(g_2y_2)),\ k \cdot (w(g_1y_1) + w(a_1c_1)) - w(a_1g_1) + k \cdot w(g_2y_2)\right\}$$

Therefore, the remaining partial weight of value $w(y_1y_2) - k \cdot w(g_2y_2)$ that g_1y_1 has to take as charge for preventing y_1y_2 satisfies the properties (I) or (II) of Lemma 7 which was covered by Case 1 or 2 above. $\square$

Using Lemma 8 and Lemma 9, we can prove our main theorem.

Proof of Theorem 6: Let M be M_m, i.e., the final solution of the algorithm. The weight of the optimal matching can be splitted as

$$w(M^*) = w(M^* \cap M) + w(M^* \setminus M)$$

The weight $w(M^* \setminus M)$ is found as charge distributed among the edges in M by a) of Lemma 8. Because no two edges in M^* share a vertex, for every $xy \in M^* \cap M$ it is $coe(xy, x) = coe(xy, y) = 0$. Therefore, xy is charged with at most $w(xy) \cdot k/(k-1)$ by c) of Lemma 8. It follows that

$$w(M^* \setminus M) \leq \sum_{xy \in M^* \cap M} \frac{k}{k-1} \cdot w(xy) + \sum_{uv \in M \setminus M^*} T(uv)$$

and we can estimate

$$w(M^*) \leq \sum_{xy \in M^* \cap M} \left(\frac{k}{k-1} + 1\right) \cdot w(xy) + \sum_{uv \in M \setminus M^*} T(uv)$$

$$\leq \left(k + \frac{k}{k-1} + \frac{k^3 - k + 1}{k^2}\right) \cdot w(M)$$

by d) of Lemma 9. □

The term describing the approximation ratio of the algorithm reaches its minimum for k being around 1.717, that yields a ratio of 5.585. It is easy to see that the algorithm does not exceed the space restriction of the semi-streaming model: It needs to memorize the edges of M and for each of those at most two shadow-edges; thus, it suffices to store a linear number of edges. The time required to handle a single input edge is determined by the size of S. Since S is of constant size, a single run of the while loop, including the enumeration and comparison of all possible augmenting sets of S, can be done in constant time. Therefore, the algorithm needs a per-edge processing time of $\mathcal{O}(1)$ and is content with a single pass over the input.

5.4 Closure

There are instances known on which the algorithm of McGregor [McG05] cannot undercut its proven approximation ratio of $2k + k/(k-1)$. Hence, this algorithm is tightly analyzed and really outperformed by our Shadow Matching algorithm for which we attested an improved ratio.

Unfortunately, we are not aware of an instance on which our algorithm does not undercut the certified ratio. We do not know if the presented analysis is tight. That leaves open two ways to further beat down the approximation ratio for the maximum weighted matching problem in the semi-streaming model: Our analysis might allow an improvement; our algorithm definitely does.

Some possible improvements of our algorithm suggest itself. It is reasonable to assume that by storing more than just two shadow-edges per matching edge and by examining more than seven edges for every input edge a superior ratio is obtainable. However, for proving such a ratio a novel approach might be required as we do not consider our different case distinctions as the appropriate way of investigating a more involved algorithm.

Chapter 6

Cuts in Graphs

6.1 Introduction

Let $G = (V, E)$ be an undirected simple graph with edges that can be unweighted or weighted. If the edges are weighted, we assume every weight to be larger than zero. A *cut* (V_1, V_2) is a partition of the vertices V into two nonempty sets V_1 and V_2. An edge uv *crosses* the cut if one endvertex of uv is in V_1 while the other one is in V_2. We denote by $|(V_1, V_2)|$ the *value* of the cut (V_1, V_2) which is the total number (or the total weight) of the edges crossing the cut.

The *minimum cut problem* is to find a minimum cut in G, that is, a cut of minimum value. We denote this value by c. Correspondingly, the *maximum cut problem* asks for a cut of maximum value; we name this value $\hat{c}$.

Note that the following definition of the approximation ratio slightly differs for the maximization and the minimization problem. Corresponding to the definition for the maximization problem in Chapter 5, we define the ratio for an algorithm approximating a maximum cut: Such an algorithm yields an α-*approximation* ratio if for every graph it computes a cut of value at least $\hat{c}/\alpha$. By contrast, an algorithm for the minimum cut problem achieves an α-*ratio* if for every graph it finds a cut of value at most $\alpha \cdot c$. This diverse definitions make sure that the ratio is always at least one and that a smaller ratio outperforms a larger one.

The semi-streaming model allows a working memory of $\mathcal{O}(n \cdot \text{polylog } n)$ bits which is $\mathcal{O}(n \log^s n)$ for some constant s. In this chapter we prefer the second notation to expose s. That way we can point out how the properties of the presented algorithms depend on their memory consumption.

Finally, we say that an event occurs *with high probability* if its probability is $1 - \mathcal{O}(n^{-\Omega(1)})$ and use *whp* to abbreviate this. Note that our definition of high probability differs from one alternatively used where the desired probability is $1 - o(1)$. However, since our definition is stronger, our results hold with respect to the alternative definition as well.

The presented work is the first to approach minimum or maximum cuts in the streaming context. The problem of minimizing a cut is covered in Section 6.2. We will see that the exact computation of a minimum cut is not possible for a one-pass streaming algorithm using $o(n^2)$ bits of working memory. We develop randomized approximation algorithms that work for different values of c and achieve different ratios. The maximum cut problem is tackled in

Section 6.3. We present an intractability result and formulate a randomized approximation algorithm. We give some closing remarks in Section 6.4.

6.2 Minimum Cut

The first traditional RAM model algorithm that approach the minimum cut problem is due to Ford and Fulkerson [FF56]. It uses the duality between a minimum cut that separates the vertices s and t from each other on the one hand and the maximum flow from s to t on the other hand. The minimum cut reflects the connectivity structure of the graph and can be used to cluster the vertices. An example for the usage of minimum cuts is given by [Bot93] where documents that are linked via a hypertext system are clustered into topically related groups.

The currently fastest algorithm to compute a minimum cut in the traditional RAM model is due to Gabow [Gab95]. It requires a running time of $\mathcal{O}(m + c^2 n \log(n/c))$ and uses a space of $\mathcal{O}(m)$. Such an exact computation is out of reach for a semi-streaming algorithm as is shown by the following section. Note that we assume the graph to be unweighted in the next sections. We give a generalization of the results about approximating a minimum cut to weighted graphs in Section 6.2.5.

6.2.1 Intractability

For a minimum cut in an unweighted graph, we will show its intractability not only for a one-pass semi-streaming algorithm. In fact, we will prove the intractability for every streaming algorithm, i.e., every algorithm that gets the graph stream as an input, that uses only one pass over the input, and has a working memory of $o(n^2)$ bits.

To this aim we make use of the theory of *communication complexity*. As only a restricted setting of this theory is utilized, the reader is referred to Kushilevitz and Nisan [KN06] for a comprehensive overview. Let X, Y, and Z be finite sets and $f : X \times Y \to Z$ be a function. There are two players, Alice and Bob, such that Alice is given an $x \in X$ and Bob is given an $y \in Y$. They want to compute $f(x, y)$ but since Alice does not know y and Bob does not know x, they have to communicate, that is, to exchange bits according to some agreed-upon communication protocol depending on f. Such a protocol tells each of the players depending on the own input and the received communication so far what message to send next. The *cost of a protocol* is the number of bits that have to be exchanged to evaluate f in the worst case, i.e, that is maximized over all inputs (x, y).

We consider the problem of *bit vector probing* where Alice knows a bit-vector x of length ℓ and Bob has an index $1 \leq i \leq \ell$. Bob wants to know x_i, that is, the ith bit of x but the communication is only allowed from Alice to Bob, not in the opposite direction. It is known [KN06] that every protocol that enables Bob to detect x_i is of cost ℓ, that is, requires the communication of the entire vector in the worst case.

The approach to exploit lower bounds of communication complexity to show lower bounds on the memory consumption for streaming computations has been used for example by Henzinger et al. [HRR99] and Ganguly and Saha [GS06]. The rough idea is to point out how a streaming algorithm using a small working memory can be used to create for a problem of communication

6.2. Minimum Cut

complexity a protocol whose cost contradicts a known lower bound. We follow this idea to prove the next theorem.

Theorem 10 *Any one-pass streaming algorithm which is able to find a minimum cut in every graph requires $\Omega(n^2)$ bits of working memory.*

Proof. Let A be a one-pass streaming algorithm using $o(n^2)$ bits of working memory that computes a minimum cut in every graph. We will use A to construct a protocol of cost $o(n^2)$ that solves the bit vector probing problem of communication complexity.

Let Alice have a bit vector x of length $(n^2 - n)/2$. She interprets this vector as the upper half of the adjacency matrix of the graph $G = (V, E)$ on n vertices. After feeding the edges of G into A, she sends the memory configuration of A to Bob followed by a sequence containing the degree of every vertex in G. Since A's memory configuration comprises of $o(n^2)$ bits and $\mathcal{O}(n \log n)$ bits suffice to transmit the vertex degrees, a total of $o(n^2)$ bits are sent from Alice to Bob.

Bob regards his index i, $1 \leq i \leq (n^2 - n)/2$, as an edge ab whose existence in G he wants to probe. He continues the execution of A by feeding more edges into it, thereby extending G to $G^+ = (V^+, E^+)$ with $V \subsetneq V^+$ and $E \subsetneq E^+$. In particular, Bob adds two disjoint cliques S and T, each of size $3n$ into G where $(S \cup T) \cap V = \emptyset$. Additionally, Bob connects every vertex in $V \setminus \{a, b\}$ to every vertex in T and both a and b to every vertex in S. Define $L := S \cup \{a, b\}$ and $R := T \cup V \setminus \{a, b\}$. Finally, Bob joins a vertex c, $c \notin \{L \cup R\}$, to $d_G(a) + d_G(b) - 1$ vertices in R where $d_G(v)$ denotes the degree of the vertex v in G. Note that $d_G(a) + d_G(b) \geq 2$ since otherwise Bob knows immediately that ab cannot be present in G.

Due to the high connectivity within each of L and R, every cut in G^+ that separates two vertices in L (R, respectively) from each other is of value at least $3n - 1$. There are only two cuts of smaller value in G^+, namely $C_1 := (L, R \cup \{c\})$ and $C_2 := (L \cup R, \{c\})$, both have a value that cannot exceed $2n$.

Now Bob can ask A for the minimum cut of G^+ to decide the existence of ab in G: If ab is in G the minimum cut of G^+ is given by C_1 of value $d_G(a) + d_G(b) - 2$. Otherwise, $|C_1| = d_G(a) + d_G(b)$ and C_2 is the minimum cut in G^+.

At the end, a one-pass streaming algorithm using $o(n^2)$ bits of memory that computes a minimum cut of every graph could be used to design a communication protocol transmitting $o(n^2)$ bits that solves the bit vector probing problem on a vector of $\Theta(n^2)$ bits. That contradicts the lower bound of $\Omega(n^2)$ bits whose communication is required in the worst case [KN06].

Note that not only the structures of the two possible minimum cuts C_1 and C_2 differ but also do their values. A one-pass streaming algorithm computing only the value of the minimum cut without its partition suffices for Bob to detect ab in G. Thus, for such an algorithm the same lower bound holds. □

The area of communication complexity also considers randomized protocols. Such protocols define the message to send next not only depending on the own input string and the received communication so far but also take random variables $r_1, r_2, \ldots$ into account. Thus, the communication itself on a given input (x, y) is not fixed anymore but becomes a random variable instead. The cost of a randomized protocol is the worst case over all inputs and choices of the r_i.

The knowledge about randomized protocols allows us to extend the result of Theorem 10 to randomized streaming algorithms.

Corollary 11 *Any randomized one-pass streaming algorithm which succeeds to find a minimum cut in every graph with a probability greater than $1/2$ requires $\Omega(n^2)$ bits of working memory.*

Proof. On the same lines as in the proof of Theorem 10, we can use a randomized one-pass streaming algorithm with $o(n^2)$ bits of working memory and success probability p to construct a randomized communication protocol of cost $o(n^2)$ with the same success probability. However, it is known [KN06] that every protocol solving the bit vector probing problem on a $\Theta(n^2)$ bit vector correctly with a probability larger than $1/2$ must be of cost $\Omega(n^2)$. □

The highly developed tool of communication complexity allows us to deduce intractability results for deterministic as well as for randomized streaming algorithms. However, the reasons for this intractability might be considered as being hidden within the communication complexity arguments. Therefore, in the next section we give an alternative proof of the intractability of a minimum cut that does not rely on communication complexity. For every one-pass streaming algorithm A using $o(n^2)$ bits we prove the existence of a graph for which A computes a wrong minimum cut. Admittedly, this appproach does not lead to an evidence about randomized streaming algorithms.

6.2.1.1 An Alternative Proof

For a graph G on labeled vertices $V = \{v_1, v_2, \ldots, v_n\}$ we define the *degree sequence* to be the sequence $d(v_1), d(v_2), \ldots, d(v_n)$ where $d(v_i)$ denotes the degree of the vertex v_i in G.

Lemma 12 *Given a family $\mathcal{G}$ containing $2^{\Omega(n^2)}$ graphs on the same n labeled vertices. Let A be a one-pass streaming algorithm using $o(n^2)$ bits of working memory. For every such A there are two graphs $G_1, G_2 \in \mathcal{G}$ that have the same degree sequence and the memory configuration of A after reading G_1 and G_2 is the same.*

Proof. For any algorithm A consider the partition $P_A(\mathcal{G})$ of $\mathcal{G}$ into sets such that all graphs within one set result in the same memory configuration when read by A. We amplify A with a self-contained routine that computes the degree sequence of the input graph by simply increasing a counter for every endvertex of an input edge. We call this amplified algorithm A^+ and note that this detection of the degree sequence can simply be done in an additional number of $\mathcal{O}(n \log n)$ bits; thus, the working memory of A^+ still contains $o(n^2)$ bits. Now observe $P_{A^+}(\mathcal{G})$, i.e., the partition of $\mathcal{G}$ into sets of graphs leading to the same memory configuration of A^+. Clearly, all graphs within one set of $P_{A^+}(\mathcal{G})$ have a common degree sequence. Since the number of sets of $P_{A^+}(\mathcal{G})$ is smaller than the number of graphs in $\mathcal{G}$, namely $2^{o(n^2)}$ compared to $2^{\Omega(n^2)}$, there is one set in $P_{A^+}(\mathcal{G})$ containing at least two graphs. Because $P_{A^+}(\mathcal{G})$ is a refinement of $P_A(\mathcal{G})$, we can find these two graphs sharing a degree sequence within one set of $P_A(\mathcal{G})$, too. □

The preceding lemma allows us to prove the intractability result.

6.2. Minimum Cut

Theorem 13 *Any one-pass streaming algorithm which is able to find a minimum cut in every graph requires $\Omega(n^2)$ bits of working memory.*

Proof. Let A be a one-pass streaming algorithm using $o(n^2)$ bits of working memory. We will construct two graphs G_1 and G_2 that lead to the same memory configuration of A but have different minimum cuts.

Fix $V = \{v_1, v_2, \ldots, v_n\}$ as a nonempty set of n labeled vertices with $n \equiv 0 \pmod{16}$. Define $C \subset V$ as $C = \{v_1, v_2, \ldots, v_{n/8}\}$. Clearly, there are $2^{\Omega(n^2)}$ different graphs on C. By Lemma 12 we can find two graphs in this family that have a common degree sequence and lead to the same memory configuration of A. Let G_1 and G_2 be these two graphs, each extended by the isolated vertices in $V \setminus C$.

By the construction so far, A cannot tell G_1 and G_2 apart. In the following we will add the very same edges to G_1 and G_2 ensuring that the augmented graphs cannot be distinguished by A, either. However, because of the inserted edges, which will involve the isolated vertices, the augmented graphs will have different cuts of minimum value.

Split the set of isolated vertices $V \setminus C$ into two sets I and J of equal sizes. Since $G_1 \neq G_2$, we find an edge ab that is contained in G_1 but not in G_2. Define $L = \{a\} \cup I$ and $R = V \setminus (L \cup \{b\})$; thus, $J \subset R$. Make L and J each a clique by augmenting G_1 and G_2 both with the necessary edges and insert all possible edges between J and $R \setminus J$ into G_1 and G_2.

As a result, every vertex in L (and R, respectively) has at least $7n/16$ neighbors in L (R) and therefore every cut that separates two vertices in L (R) from each other has a value of at least $7n/16$. As a result, there are only three cuts in G_1 and G_2 of smaller value, in particular, $X = (L, R \cup \{b\})$, $Y = (L \cup \{b\}, R)$ and $Z = (L \cup R, \{b\})$.

Let X_1 be set of edges crossing the cut X in G_1, X_2 be the edges crossing X in G_2, correspondingly define Y_1, Y_2, Z_1, and Z_2. Let A_1 (A_2, respectively) be the set of edges going between a and R in G_1 (G_2) and B_1 (B_2) be the set of edges going between b and R in G_1 (G_2). Figure 6.1 may help to clarify the myriad of defined terms.

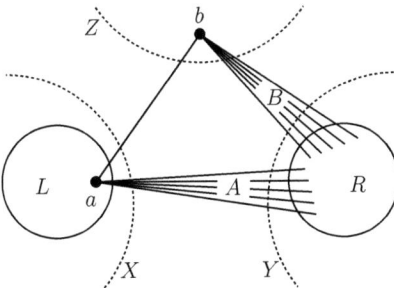

Figure 6.1: The edge ab, which is contained in G_1 but not in G_2, and the edge sets A and B cross the three possible minimum cuts X, Y, and Z in different ways.

Since the degree of a is the same in G_1 and G_2, it follows that $|X_1| = |X_2|$ and because ab is not in G_2, it is $|A_2| = |A_1| + 1$. Similarly, the degree of b in G_1 equals that in G_2, so $|Z_1| = |Z_2|$

and thus $|B_2| = |B_1|+1$. Because $|Y_1| = |A_1|+|B_1|$ and $|Y_2| = |A_2|+|B_2|$, we have $|Y_2| = |Y_1|+2$. Hence, the value of the cut Y in G_2 exceeds the value of the cut Y in G_1 by two.

Observe that $|Y_2| = |A_2| + |B_2| = |X_2| + |Z_2|$ and because by construction $|X_2| > 0$ and $|Z_2| > 0$, we have $|Y_2| > |X_2|$ and $|Y_2| > |Z_2|$. Thus, we can find a $k \geq 0$ such that

$$\min\{|X_2|+k, |Z_2|+k\} = \min\{|X_1|+k, |Z_1|+k\} = |Y_2| - 1$$

Since $|X_2| < n/8$ and $|Z_2| < n/8$, k must be smaller than $n/8$, too.

Because $|L \setminus \{a\}| = 7n/16$, we can take k vertices from $L \setminus \{a\}$ and add an edge between every such vertex and b to both G_1 and G_2. As a result, $|X_1|, |X_2|, |Z_1|$, and $|Z_2|$ each increase by k while $|Y_1|$ and $|Y_2|$ remain unaffected.

Finally, $\min\{|X_1|, |Z_1|\} = \min\{|X_2|, |Z_2|\} = |Y_1| + 1 = |Y_2| - 1 < n/4$. Therefore, the cut of minimum value in G_1 is Y while in G_2 it is the smaller one of X and Z. Note also that not only the minimum cuts in G_1 and G_2 disagree but also their respective values differ by one.

It is easy to choose the order of the edges of G_1 and G_2 in the corresponding input streams for the algorithm A in such a way that after reading the stream of G_1 the memory configuration of A is the very same as after reading the stream of G_2: The first part of the streams each consists of the edges from the initial composition on C. After reading this first part, which is different for G_1 and G_2, the memory configuration of A will be the same for both streams by construction. The second part of the input streams is provided by the edges added into L, into R, and between $L \setminus \{a\}$ and b. Because this second part of the input streams is the same for G_1 and G_2, the whole input streams both will lead to the same memory configuration of A. Therefore, A gives the same answer on the input streams of G_1 and G_2 making a mistake for at most one of them. □

6.2.2 Calculating Small Minimum Cuts

Even though the minimum cut problem is intractable in general for a semi-streaming algorithm, the special case of a small minimum cut is easier to solve. If the minimum cut value c of a graph G is known to be smaller than $k = \log^s n$ for some constant s, it is feasible to find a minimum cut of G in the semi-streaming model: As pointed out in Section 4.2.4, a certificate G' for k-edge connectivity of G can be computed. It consists of kn edges and reflects the connectivity structure of G. In particular, G' is generated by a method proposed by Nagamochi and Ibaraki [NI92] in such a way that every cut in G' of value smaller than k is a cut of the same value in G. G' can be computed using a constant per-edge processing time and examining it in a postprocessing step reveals a minimum cut of G and its value. For the postprocessing step, we can use the currently fastest minimum cut algorithm of Gabow [Gab95] whose running time on G' reduces to $\mathcal{O}(n \log^{2s+1} n)$. However, if Gabow's algorithm certifies G' to be k-edge connected, this approach fails since c is of value at least k.

6.2.3 Approximating Large Minimum Cuts

If the minimum cut value is larger than $\log^s n$, we know that G must consist of $\Omega(n \log^s n)$ edges. To approach such cuts we utilize *randomized sparsification* as presented by Karger [Kar94]. For

6.2. MINIMUM CUT

an input graph G this method constructs a subgraph G_p, that is, a graph on the same vertices including each edge of G independently with probability p. Intuitively, we expect that the minimum cut in G_p corresponds to a cut in G whose value is close to the minimum cut value of G. The next theorem validates this intuition.

Theorem 14 (Karger [Kar94]) *Let G be a graph with minimum cut of value c and let $p \geq 54 \ln n / (\varepsilon^2 c)$ for some constant $\varepsilon > 0$. Let D be a minimum cut in G_p that is of value $|D|_{G_p}$ in G_p and of value $|D|$ in G. Then with high probability*

$$|D| \leq (1+\varepsilon) \cdot c \quad \text{and} \quad (1-\varepsilon) \cdot |D| \leq |D|_{G_p}/p \leq (1+\varepsilon) \cdot |D|$$

Note that if the partition of the vertices is concerned, a minimum cut in G and a minimum cut G_p might fundamentally differ. The above theorem only states that their values in G are close. Additionally, the theorem allows a good estimation of $|D|$ and c by dividing $|D|_{G_p}$ by p.

The theorem's utilization for a semi-streaming algorithm is obvious: Each edge in the input stream is independently chosen to be memorized by the algorithm with probability p. After reading all edges, the minimum cut of the stored graph G_p is computed. This cut gives an $(1 + \varepsilon)$-approximate solution for the original graph and allows an estimation of c.

For this approach p must be fixed at the start of the algorithm. Theorem 14, however, only works for graphs whose minimum cut value exceeds a value depending on p and ε. Since for decreasing p this value increases, it is desirable to fix p as being large to make the theorem applicable for as many graphs as possible.

On the other hand, a large p implies a large number of edges in G_p. But G_p can only consist of $\mathcal{O}(n \log^s n)$ edges for some constant s to be storable within the working memory of a semi-streaming algorithm. As a result, p is best chosen to be $\Theta(n \log^s n/m)$. By applying the Chernoff bounds in the following Theorem 15, it is easy to see that whp G_p then contains $\Theta(n \log^s n)$ edges and fits into the working memory.

If n and m are known to the algorithm before the input stream arrives, p is easy to compute. However, we are not aware of a technique enabling a semi-steaming algorithm to sample $\Theta(n \log^s n)$ edges uniformly from the input stream without knowing n in advance.

If n but not m is known beforehand, we can use the following approach of *reservoir sampling* introduced by Vitter [Vit85]. The first $n \log^s n$ edges in the input stream are stored as the reservoir in the algorithm's working memory. If an edge e at position $t > n \log^s n$ in the input stream arrives, e is inserted into the reservoir with a probability of $n \log^s n/t$ and thereby replaces an edge in the reservoir chosen uniformly at random. After reading the whole input stream, the reservoir consists of $n \log^s n$ edges, each of them sampled independently with probability $n \log^s n/m$.

Now we can specify the semi-streaming algorithm that tries to utilize Karger's approach in Theorem 14 to approximate a minimum cut in G. At the start the algorithm is given n and ε. If additionally m is given to the algorithm, it computes $p = n \log^s n/m$ and samples the input edges with probability p. Otherwise, reservoir sampling is used. In either case, that results in the graph G_p having $\Theta(n \log^s n)$ edges whp and p being $n \log^s n/m$.

After reading all edges with a per-edge processing time of $\mathcal{O}(1)$, the algorithm computes a minimum cut in the sampled graph G_p of value c_p in G_p. Using Gabow's algorithm [Gab95] this yields a postprocessing time of $\mathcal{O}(n \log^s n + c_p^2 n \log(n/c_p))$. If $c_p \geq (1+\alpha) \cdot 54 \ln n/\varepsilon^2$ for some small constant $\alpha > 0$, the minimum cut of G_p and c_p/p is given as a solution and its estimated value in G.

If otherwise c_p is smaller, the algorithm fails. Theorem 14 is not applicable anymore since p is likely to be too small compared to c and ε.

To certify this approach in Lemma 16, we need to estimate the probability of a binomially distributed random variable deviating from its expectation. For this we use the Chernoff bound, originally mentioned in [Che52], in the following formulations.

Theorem 15 ([JLR00]) *Let X be a binomially distributed random variable on s trials with success probability p and expected number of successes $\mathbb{E}[X] = sp$. For $t \geq 0$*

$$\mathbb{P}[X \geq \mathbb{E}[X] + t] \leq \exp\left\{-\frac{t^2}{2(\mathbb{E}[X] + t/3)}\right\} \tag{6.1}$$

$$\mathbb{P}[X \leq \mathbb{E}[X] - t] \leq \exp\left\{-\frac{t^2}{2\mathbb{E}[X]}\right\} \tag{6.2}$$

Lemma 16 *If $c_p \geq (1+\alpha) \cdot 54 \ln n/\varepsilon^2$, then with high probability $p > 54 \ln n/(\varepsilon^2 c)$.*

Proof. We bound the probability that all cuts in G of value at most $54 \ln n/(p\varepsilon^2)$ induce a cut of value at least $(1+\alpha) \cdot 54 \ln n/\varepsilon^2$ in G_p. This probability is bounded by the probability that this occurs to a single cut D whose value is at most $54 \ln n/(p\varepsilon^2)$. Let X_D be the value of D in G_p and note that $\mathbb{E}[X_D] \leq 54 \ln n/\varepsilon^2$. Together with the Chernoff bound (6.1) we can deduce:

$$\begin{aligned}
\mathbb{P}[X_D \geq (1+\alpha) \cdot 54 \ln n/\varepsilon^2] &\leq \mathbb{P}[X_D \geq \mathbb{E}[X_D] + \alpha \cdot 54 \ln n/\varepsilon^2] \\
&\leq \exp\left\{-\frac{(\alpha \cdot 54 \ln n/\varepsilon^2)^2}{2(\mathbb{E}[X_D] + \alpha \cdot 54 \ln n/3\varepsilon^2)}\right\} \\
&\leq \exp\left\{-\frac{81\alpha^2 \cdot \ln n}{(3+\alpha)\varepsilon^2}\right\} \\
&= n^{-\Omega(1)}
\end{aligned}$$

Accordingly, if $c_p \geq (1+\alpha) \cdot 54 \ln n/\varepsilon^2$, whp there is no cut of value at most $54 \ln n/(p\varepsilon^2)$ in G. Thus, $c > 54 \ln n/(p\varepsilon^2)$ and $p > 54 \ln n/(c\varepsilon^2)$. □

As a result, if c_p is big enough, the used sample probability p whp meets the demand of Theorem 14 which assures the correctness of the algorithm.

Finally, we can $(1+\varepsilon)$-approximate a minimum cut on all graphs whose minimum cut value is $\Omega(m/(n \log^{s-1} n))$: By choosing a suitable sampling probability $p = \Theta(n \log^s n/m)$, the requirement of Theorem 14 is met. The Theorem then assures that whp the minimum cut

6.2. MINIMUM CUT

in G_p satisfies the condition of Lemma 16 which causes the algorithm to output a solution. This solution, again by Theorem 14, is a $(1+\varepsilon)$-approximate solution for the input graph.

By an easy application of the Cherhoff bound (6.1), the sampled graph G_p does not exceed the memory restriction of the semi-streaming model which allows the memorization of $\mathcal{O}(n \log^s n)$ edges.

6.2.4 Approximating Medium-sized Minimum Cuts

To deal with minimum cuts whose value is too small to utilize Theorem 14 we use a different approach of Karger [Kar94] the concept of which we roughly sketch in the following. The idea is to figure out a probability q such that randomly removing each edge in G independently with probability q causes G to become disconnected with some specific probability p_d.

To this aim, G is duplicated to get identical copies G_j of G for $j = 1, 2, \ldots, n^\delta \log n$ for some δ. To every edge in each of the $n^\delta \log n$ copies of G a random weight in the unit interval is assigned. Now a spanning tree T_j of maximum weight is computed in each G_j. The weight of the minimum weight edge in T_j is called $w(G_j)$, the $(\log n)$th smallest value of all the $w(G_j)$ is named q. If every edge in G is removed with a probability q, G gets disconnected with probability $p_d = \Theta(n^{-\delta})$. This relation allows an estimation of c since the random edge removals disconnect G most likely at a minimum cut. Karger [Kar94] shows that the calculation of $\sqrt{\delta(2+\delta)} \cdot \log_{1/q} n$ gives an approximation of c. The partition of V induced by deleting the edge of weight q in its maximum spanning tree specifies the corresponding cut in G.

Theorem 17 (Karger [Kar94]) *With the use of $\mathcal{O}(n^\delta \log n)$ independent trials of randomly assigning weights in the unit interval to the edges of G and computing the minimum weight edge in a maximum spanning tree, the minimum cut of G can be approximated with high probability to a factor of $\sqrt{1+2/\delta}$.*

In Section 4.2.5 we proposed a semi-streaming algorithm computing a minimum spanning tree of a graph storing at most $\mathcal{O}(n \log n)$ edges. By simply inverting the result of comparing two edges, this algorithm calculates a maximum spanning tree. If to every edge in the input stream a random weight in the unit interval is assigned, the algorithm calculates $w(G)$, that is, the weight of a minimum weight edge of a maximum weighted spanning tree. If $n \log^s n$ of those weighted edges for some constant s can be memorized by a semi-streaming algorithm, such an algorithm can execute $\log^{s-1} n$ independent trials of assigning edge weights and computing $w(G)$ in parallel. This corresponds to setting $\delta = \log \log^{s-1} n / \log n$ in Theorem 17, thus whp gives an approximation of ratio $\sqrt{1 + 2 \log n / \log \log^{s-1} n}$.

The constant per-edge processing time and the postprocessing time of $\mathcal{O}(n \log n)$ are both inherited from the used algorithm of Section 4.2.5. This postprocessing time also suffices to find q, to calculate the estimation of c, and to find the partition specifying the approximative minimum cut.

Of course, we cannot store an edge weighted with an arbitrary real from $[0, 1]$ in the memory constraint of the semi-streaming model. Instead, we assume every single weight to be storable within $\mathcal{O}(\text{polylog } n)$ bits. Such a weight can be seen as a rounded weight from one in $[0, 1]$. The usage of rounded weights instead of real ones increases the approximation ratio in Theorem 17 only in a negligible way.

6.2.5 Generalization

The three approaches estimating a minimum cut of G in the semi-streaming model can be joined to an algorithm A which simply runs the three approaches in parallel. If after reading all edges the first method detects a minimum cut of value at most $\log^s n$, A outputs this cut and its value as an exact solution. If the first approach fails, that is, if G is $(\log^s n)$-edge connected, the result of the second approach is of interest. If it does not fail, it gives a $(1 + \varepsilon)$-approximative solution whp. If the first and the second approach cannot give a solution, A outputs the one of the third approach, which whp is an approximation of ratio $\sqrt{1 + 2\log n / \log\log^{s-1} n}$. As a result, A estimates a minimum cut of general value in G with high probability achieving an approximation ratio depending on c.

All three approaches admit a generalization to edge weighted graphs. If the weights are integers, the algorithm, when reading an input edge e of weight $w(e)$, can simply regard this as reading $w(e)$ parallel unweighted edges. The per-edge processing time increases by a factor of $w(e)$. Note that m, instead of denoting the number of the input edges, now indicates the total sum of the edge weights. Since the algorithm of Gabow [Gab95] used in the postprocessing step of the second approach also works on multigraphs, we can still use it to find a minimum cut in the sampled G_p which might have parallel edges now.

For the general case of non-integral weights, the algorithm can round every weight after scaling it with a large constant. That certainly increases the error in the approximation ratio but by choosing this constant large enough, the introduced error is insignificant.

6.3 Maximum Cut

The maximum cut problem is one of Karp's original $\mathcal{NP}$-complete problems [Kar72] and even for unweighted graphs this hardness is known [GJ90]. While achieving a $(1.0625 - \varepsilon)$-approximation is $\mathcal{NP}$-complete for every $\varepsilon > 0$ [Hås01], the algorithm due to Goemanns and Williamson [GW95] producing a 1.1383-ratio is the best known approximation algorithm. This ratio is believed to be tight by a result of Khot et al. [KKMO04]. In addition to its theoretical importance, the maximum cut problem has applications in the design of circuit layouts and in statistical physics, cf. [BGJR88].

6.3.1 Intractability

In order to prove the intractability of the maximum cut problem for a one-pass streaming algorithm, we need the following technical lemma.

Lemma 18 *Let H be a graph on the vertex classes L and R with $|L| = |R| = 5n - 1$ and let $L' \subsetneq L$ and $R' \subsetneq R$ be both of size n with $n > 0$. An edge uv is in H if and only if*

- $u \in L$ and $v \in R$,
- $u, v \in L'$, or

6.3. Maximum Cut

- $u, v \in R'$.

Then any cut in H differing from (L, R) is at most of value $|L| \cdot |R| - 4n + 1$.

Proof. Starting from the cut (L, R) of value $|L| \cdot |R|$, we can produce any other cut by exchanging vertices in $A \subseteq L$ with vertices in $B \subseteq R$. We can assume that $|A| + |B| \leq 5n - 1$ since otherwise $|L \setminus A| + |R \setminus B| < 5n - 1$ whose exchange produces the same cut. After moving A to R, we can roughly estimate the value of the resulting cut $(L \setminus A, R \cup A)$ to be smaller than $|L| \cdot |R| - |A|(5n - 1) + |A|n$. After moving B to $L \setminus A$, the resulting cut is of value smaller than

$$|L| \cdot |R| - |A| \cdot (5n - 1) + |A| \cdot n - |B| \cdot (5n - 1 - |A|) + |B| \cdot n + |A| \cdot |B|$$

which equals $|L| \cdot |R| + |A|(|B| - 4n + 1) + |B|(|A| - 4n + 1)$. For $|A|, |B| \geq 0$ and $0 < |A| + |B| \leq 5n - 1$ this term takes its maximum with $|A| + |B| = 1$ at a value of $|L| \cdot |R| - 4n + 1$. □

Now we can show the very same result for the maximum cut problem as we did for the minimization problem.

Theorem 19 *Any one-pass streaming algorithm finding a maximum cut in every graph requires $\Omega(n^2)$ bits of working memory.*

Proof. The proof is very similar to the one of Theorem 10 showing the intractability of the minimum cut problem, so we borrow the framework of the proof from there. Remember that Bob receives the memory configuration of the streaming algorithm after reading $G = (V, E)$, which is only known to Alice, followed by the degree of every vertex. Again, Bob wants to probe the edge ab in G.

To this aim he extends G to obtain G^+. In contrast to the proof of Theorem 10, Bob adds a complete bipartite graph on the color classes L and Q with $(L \cup Q) \cap V = \emptyset$ and $|L| = 5n - 1$, $|Q| = 4n + 1$. He connects every vertex in $V \setminus \{a, b\}$ to every vertex in L and joins vertex a to $d_G(a) - 1$ vertices in L and b to $d_G(b) - 1$ vertices in L. It must be $d_G(a) > 0$ and $d_G(b) > 0$ since otherwise Bob knows directly that ab is not in G.

We define $R := Q \cup V \setminus \{a, b\}$; thus, $|L| = |R| = 5n - 1$. Note that the subgraph of G^+ induced on L and R is a subgraph of the graph constructed in Lemma 18.

Because each of a and b had at most $n - 1$ neighbors in G and gained at most $n - 2$ new neighbors in G^+, the sum of the degrees of a and b in G^+ is at most $4n - 6$. Therefore, with Lemma 18 we can deduce that any cut in G^+ that does not separate the vertices in L from those in R is of value at most $|L| \cdot |R| - 5$ even if all edges incident to a or b are crossing edges.

As a result, we get a maximum cut in G^+ when separating L from R and by adding a and b each to L or R. Where a and b are placed in a maximum cut, depends on the existence of ab in G.

If ab is in G then a (b, respectively) has the same number of neighbors in L and R. Then every maximum cut separates a from b to make ab a crossing edge. If ab is not in G then the number of a's (b's) neighbors in R exceeds the number of a's (b's) neighbors in L by one. Thus, the maximum cut is given by $(L \cup \{a,b\}, R)$.

Bob can probe the existence of ab in G by asking the one-pass streaming algorithm for the maximum cut of G^+. If the algorithm was content with $o(n^2)$ bits of working memory that gives rise to a communication protocol solving the bit vector probing problem with cost $o(n^2)$. This contradicts the lower bound of $\Omega(n^2)$ for the cost of every protocol tackling this problem if Alice holds a vector of length $\Theta(n^2)$ [KN06].

As in the proof of Theorem 10, the value of the maximum cut in G^+ differs depending on the presence of ab in G. Hence, for any one-pass streaming algorithm computing this value without yielding a partition, the proved lower bound holds as well. □

We can deduce a lower bound for a randomized algorithm in the very same way as we did in Corollary 11.

Corollary 20 *Any randomized one-pass streaming algorithm which succeeds to find a maximum cut in every graph with a probability larger than $1/2$ requires $\Omega(n^2)$ bits of working memory.*

Corresponding to the minimization problem, it is possible to prove the intractability of a maximum cut for a deterministic streaming algorithm A using $o(n^2)$ bits without communication complexity. Similar to the proof of Theorem 13, two graphs with different maximum cuts can be constructed that cannot be told apart by A.

6.3.2 Approximating Maximum Cut

In this section we give two randomized semi-streaming algorithms approximating a maximum cut. Again, we restrict G to be unweighted first before we give a generalization to weighted graphs in Section 6.3.3. The algorithm achieving a 2-approximation is trivial and only presented to point out the different nature of the maximum cut problem opposed to the minimization problem where to obtain a constant factor approximation seems much harder. We will only sketch the proof bounding the trivial algorithm's error probability because the second algorithm yielding a superior $(1+\varepsilon)$-approximation will be presented afterwards.

The randomized semi-streaming algorithm computing a 2-approximation of a maximum cut is based on an observation of Sahni and Gonzales [SG76]. When the algorithm encounters a vertex v for the first time as an endvertex of an input edge, the algorithm puts v into one of two sets A and B with equal probability. Now the algorithm can count the number of edges crossing the cut (A, B) and finally outputs this cut and its exact value as the solution. Because every edge crosses the cut with probability $1/2$ and at most all edges cross the maximum cut, the computed cut (A, B) is a randomized 2-approximation. Note that this can be achieved without knowing the number of vertices.

Certainly, storing each edge crossing the cut potentially exceeds the memory constraint. If the crossing edges are of detailed interest, the algorithm can output them as they occur producing an output stream.

6.3. MAXIMUM CUT

The required per-edge processing time is $\mathcal{O}(1)$, the algorithm is content with $\mathcal{O}(n)$ bits of working memory.

Note that we only stressed the fact that the trivial algorithm gives a 2-approximation as the expected value. To limit the algorithm's error probability, we cannot apply standard Chernoff arguments to the sum of the crossing edges since the selections of different edges into the random cut are no independent events. However, we can use such arguments to show that for every vertex v the number of crossing edges incident to v is close to $d(v)/2$ whp if $d(v) \geq \log n$. Because of that we can deduce that the trivial algorithm yields $(2+\varepsilon)$-approximation whp for any $\varepsilon > 0$ on every input graph G with at least $n \log^2 n$ edges, that is, in which the number of vertices whose degree is too small can be disregarded. If G has less edges, it can be stored completely and scanned for an optimal solution in the postprocessing step.

We will now see that the approach of randomly sampling the input edges, which is useful to approximate a minimum cut only if it exceeds a certain value, is suitable for all maximum cuts. This is due to the fact that there are no maximum cuts of small value. In particular, it holds that $\hat{c} \geq m/2$ for every graph with maximum cut value $\hat{c}$ and m edges, cf. [PT95].

The semi-streaming algorithm approximating a maximum cut starts by sampling the input graph G as described in Section 6.2.3. Remember that this results in a graph G_p in which every edge of G is sampled independently with probability $p = n \log^s n / m$. In the postprocessing step a maximum cut in G_p of value $\hat{c}_p$ is identified by a complete enumeration of all cuts in exponential time. This cut and its estimated value $\hat{c}_p/p$ in G are given as the solution.

The $(1+\varepsilon)$-approximation ratio of this algorithm which is proven in the next theorem is the best ratio possible for a semi-streaming algorithm due to Corollary 20.

Theorem 21 *Let B be a maximum cut in G_p of size $\hat{c}_p$ in G_p. To output B and $\hat{c}_p/p$ as its estimated value in G yields a $(1+\varepsilon)$-approximation of the maximum cut in G for every constant $\varepsilon > 0$ with high probability.*

Proof. We limit the probability that the algorithm misses the promised ratio, i.e., produces a cut of value smaller than $\hat{c}/(1+\varepsilon)$ in G for some $\varepsilon > 0$.

Let D be a cut whose value is smaller than $\hat{c}/(1+\varepsilon)$ and let C be a maximum cut in G. Their values in G_p we denote by X_D and X_C. Using $a := \hat{c} \cdot p/(1+\varepsilon/2)$ we can bound the probability that the algorithm outputs the cut D:

$$\begin{aligned}
\mathbb{P}[\text{ alg. outputs } D\,] &\leq \mathbb{P}[X_D \geq X_C] \\
&= \mathbb{P}[X_D \geq x \text{ and } X_C \leq x \text{ and } x < a] \quad (6.3)\\
&\quad + \mathbb{P}[X_D \geq x \text{ and } X_C \leq x \text{ and } x \geq a] \quad (6.4)
\end{aligned}$$

Part (6.3) is limited by the probability that X_C is at most $\hat{c} \cdot p/(1+\varepsilon/2)$. Since $\mathbb{E}[X_C] = \hat{c} \cdot p$, we can bound this probability by the Chernoff bound (6.2):

$$\begin{aligned}
\mathbb{P}\left[X_C \leq \frac{\hat{c} \cdot p}{1+\varepsilon/2}\right] &= \mathbb{P}\left[X_C \leq \mathbb{E}[X_C] - \frac{\hat{c} \cdot p \cdot \varepsilon}{2+\varepsilon}\right] \\
&\leq \exp\left\{-\frac{\hat{c} \cdot p \cdot \varepsilon^2}{2(2+\varepsilon)^2}\right\} \quad (6.5)
\end{aligned}$$

Part (6.4) is bounded by the probability that X_D is at least $\hat{c} \cdot p/(1+\varepsilon/2)$. With the Chernoff bound (6.1) and $\mathbb{E}[X_D] < \hat{c} \cdot p/(1+\varepsilon)$ we can deduce:

$$\mathbb{P}\left[X_D \geq \frac{\hat{c} \cdot p}{1+\varepsilon/2}\right] \leq \mathbb{P}\left[X_D \geq \mathbb{E}[X_D] + \frac{\hat{c} \cdot p \cdot \varepsilon}{2+3\varepsilon+\varepsilon^2}\right]$$

$$\leq \exp\left\{-\frac{3\hat{c} \cdot p \cdot \varepsilon^2}{24+52\varepsilon+36\varepsilon^2+8\varepsilon^3}\right\} \quad (6.6)$$

Due to $\hat{c} = \Omega(m)$ and $p = n\log^s n/m$, expressions (6.5) and (6.6) and therefore the probability that the algorithm gives D as its solution are bounded by $\exp\{-\Omega(n\log^s n)\}$. There are less than 2^n cuts whose value is more than a factor of $(1+\varepsilon)$ away from the optimal solution. Hence, the total probability that the algorithm misses the promised ratio by computing any of those small cuts is bounded by $n^{-\Omega(1)}$.

In addition to the cut B as the maximum cut in G_p, the algorithm returns $\hat{c}_p/p$ as an estimation of $|B|$, that is, the value of B in G. It is easy to see that whp $\hat{c}_p/p$ is close to the maximum cut value of G: By again utilizing the Chernoff bounds, it can be shown that whp $|B|$ is at most a $(1+\varepsilon')$-factor away from $\hat{c}_p/p$ for any constant ε'. $|B|$ in turn $(1+\varepsilon)$-approximates the maximum cut value whp as proven. □

The randomized $(1+\varepsilon)$-approximative algorithm uses an exhaustive search to find the maximum cut of G_p in the postprocessing step. This causes the postprocessing time and therefore the overall computing time to be $\Omega(2^n \cdot \text{poly}(n))$. It is interesting to note that we do not know how to reduce this time. For the semi-streaming model only an algorithm using linear space is acceptable for the postprocessing step. But even for polynomially bounded space, faster exact algorithms computing a maximum cut are unknown [Woe04]. All known faster exact algorithms require exponential space.

Even at the expense of the approximation ratio, we cannot obtain a reasonable speedup of the postprocessing step. The idea to use an approximation algorithm in the postprocessing step seems obvious. However, the algorithm of Goemanns and Williamson [GW95], which gives a 1.1383-approximation in polynomial time is not applicable. It uses a semidefinite programming approach relying on adjacency matrices that exceed the memory constraint. Apart from this, no polynomial time algorithm is known that substantially surpasses a 2-approximation. But such a 2-approximation is useless since it would not undercut the ratio of the presented trivial semi-streaming algorithm.

6.3.3 Generalization

Both algorithms presented to estimate a maximum cut can be generalized to weighted graphs. The trivial algorithm simply sums up the weights of the edges crossing the random cut. The per-edge processing time remains the same and the size of the working memory might only be increased to store the cut value.

The edge sampling algorithm can be generalized by regarding the input graph as a multigraph as described in Section 6.2.5. That causes the per-edge processing time to increase accordingly. Because $\hat{c}$ still equals at least the half of the total sum of the edge weights, the bound on the error probability in Theorem 21 persists.

6.4 Closure

In the traditional RAM-model, the complexity of the minimum cut problem fundamentally falls below the one of the maximum cut problem, provided $\mathcal{P} \neq \mathcal{NP}$. The semi-streaming model, however, does not emphasize the running time of an algorithm as the most important measure of complexity. Rather, the model focuses on the general question to which extend a problem is solvable under the shortened conditions when forbidding random access and restricting working memory.

From this streaming viewpoint, the minimum cut problem does not seem to be easier than the maximum cut problem. For both problems we proved the intractability of an accurate solution, even if randomization is allowed. While we can exactly compute small minimum cuts deterministically in the semi-streaming model, we are unable to give a randomized constant factor approximation for minimum cuts of general values. On the other hand, such an approximation is trivially obtained for the maximum cut problem. Moreover, the constitution of maximum cuts permits a randomized $(1 + \varepsilon)$-approximation by uniform sampling. The exponential postprocessing time of this algorithm is inherited from the RAM-model. This does not derogate our speculation that the maximum cut problem is easier than the minimum cut one in terms of general accessibility for streaming computations.

Chapter 7

Conclusion

This book concerned how various graph problems can be approached if the assumption of random access to the input graph G is dropped and the working memory is restricted such that the storage of the whole graph is forbidden. The precise model under consideration was that of a semi-streaming algorithm which gets a stream of G's edges in arbitrary order as an input and has a working memory limited to $\mathcal{O}(n \cdot \operatorname{polylog} n)$ bits.

In Chapter 4 we presented semi-streaming algorithms working in one pass over the input stream for computing the connected components, a bipartition, the k-vertex and k-edge connectivity for any $k = \mathcal{O}(\operatorname{polylog} n)$, and a minimum spanning forest of a given graph. For these problems semi-streaming algorithms were known before. However, all of these algorithms use a per-edge processing time that increases with the size of the input graph.

In contrast, the per-edge processing times of the algorithms we introduced are constant and therefore optimal. Moreover, all presented algorithms use an overall computing time that asymptotically equals the best known corresponding time in the traditional RAM model. For the computation of the connected components, a bipartition, and the minimum spanning forest, we actually achieved the time bounds of the fastest RAM model algorithms that are possible.

The main idea for our semi-streaming algorithms is quite simple: A sparse memorized subgraph is merged with buffered edges and while computing a sparse subgraph of the merged one, the next input edges are buffered. This approach is enabled by the existence of sparse and strong certificates for the mentioned problems. The sparseness of a certificate permits its storage within the constrained working memory while the strongness allows the iterative update step. The final certificate can be queried for the graph property in question as a substitution for the input graph.

Chapter 5 covered the problem of finding a maximum weighted matching in a graph G. It has been known before that this problem is not tractable in the semi-streaming model. Previously existing approximation algorithms for this problem are maintaining an actual matching M while reading the input stream. The weight of an input edge e determines if e replaces adjacent edges in M. We enhanced the algorithms known before which are limited to the storage of the edges in M. In addition to the edges of M, our algorithm memorizes some more edges of G; these edges we call shadow-edges. For each input edge e, the subgraph S made up of e, of some shadow-edges, and edges of M in the vicinity of e is examined. If a certain gain in the weight of M can be achieved, matching and non-matching edges in S are exchanged.

To prove the approximation ratio of our matching algorithm, a charging scheme was utilized: We assumed that every edge o of an optimal solution is charging its weight to the edges that prevent o from being inserted into M. If charged edges are replaced, the charge must be transferred. If the sum of the charges on the edges of the final M can be bounded as a multiple of the weight of the final M, this yields the approximation ratio.

The general idea of such a charging scheme has been used before to prove the ratio of the previously known algorithms for the same problem. However, these algorithms only employ simple replacement steps which make the charge transfer easy to follow. To retrace the charge transfer for our more involved replacement steps, we had to significantly enhance the charging scheme. Finally, we proved an approximation ratio of 5.585 for our algorithm which surpasses all ratios for this problem known before.

Chapter 6 dealt with the problems of finding a minimum and a maximum cut in a graph. Nothing has been known before for these problems under streaming assumptions. For both problems we proved that neither a deterministic nor a randomized streaming algorithm can solve them exactly. The proofs showed how such an algorithm could be exploited to design a protocol for a problem of communication complexity that transmits a number of bits contradicting known lower bounds.

We tackled the minimum cut problem by three different approaches that cover different values of the minimum cut and achieve different solution qualities. Small minimum cuts can be computed exactly by the deterministic method presented in Chapter 4. We showed a minimum cut of large value to be $(1+\varepsilon)$-approximable by randomly sampling the input edges. We used an approach that examines the dependency between random edge removals and the decomposition of the input graph to approximate a minimum cut of medium value.

For the maximum cut problem, it is easy to present a trivial randomized semi-streaming algorithm that achieves a $(2+\varepsilon)$-ratio with high probability. We proved a better ratio of $(1+\varepsilon)$ to be attainable with high probability by randomly sampling the input edges and computing a maximum cut of the sampled graph in the postprocessing step.

All problems under consideration in this book have been extensively studied before in the traditional RAM model which allows random access and unlimited memory. To investigate a problem in a context where these powerful assumptions are taken away, may help to understand which computational resources are really needed to make a problem easily solvable. While the problems of Chapter 4 do not benefit from random access and unlimited memory, the matching problem significantly does. The degrees of hardness of the minimum and the maximum cut problem which are believed to vary essentially in the RAM model give a different picture in the streaming context. For all approached problems, it is interesting to see how they present themselves if the point of view is changed to that of a streaming algorithm.

Bibliography

[ADRR04] Aggarwal, Gagan; Datar, Mayur; Rajagopalan, Sridhar; Ruhl, Matthias: On the streaming model augmented with a sorting primitive. In: *FOCS '04: Proceedings of the 45th Annual IEEE Symposium on Foundations of Computer Science*, pp. 540–549. IEEE Computer Society, Washington, DC, USA, 2004.

[AHU75] Aho, Alfred V.; Hopcroft, John E.; Ullman, Jeffrey D.: *The design and analysis of computer algorithms*. Addison-Wesley Publishing Co., Reading, Mass.-London-Amsterdam, 1975.

[AMS96] Alon, Noga; Matias, Yossi; Szegedy, Mario: The space complexity of approximating the frequency moments. In: *STOC '96: Proceedings of the twenty-eighth annual ACM symposium on Theory of computing*, pp. 20–29. ACM, New York, NY, USA, 1996.

[BAJ00] Barabasi, Albert-Laszlo; Albert, Reka; Jeong, Hawoong: Scale-free characteristics of random networks: the topology of the world-wide web. In: *Physica A: Statistical Mechanics and its Applications*, volume 281(1-4):pp. 69–77, 2000.

[Bas08] Baswana, Surender: Streaming algorithm for graph spanners—single pass and constant processing time per edge. In: *Inf. Process. Lett.*, volume 106(3):pp. 110–114, 2008.

[BBD+02] Babcock, Brian; Babu, Shivnath; Datar, Mayur; Motwani, Rajeev; Widom, Jennifer: Models and issues in data stream systems. In: *PODS '02: Proceedings of the twenty-first ACM SIGMOD-SIGACT-SIGART symposium on Principles of database systems*, pp. 1–16. ACM, New York, NY, USA, 2002.

[BFL+06] Buriol, Luciana S.; Frahling, Gereon; Leonardi, Stefano; Marchetti-Spaccamela, Alberto; Sohler, Christian: Counting triangles in data streams. In: *PODS '06: Proceedings of the twenty-fifth ACM SIGMOD-SIGACT-SIGART symposium on Principles of database systems*, pp. 253–262. ACM, New York, NY, USA, 2006.

[BGJR88] Barahona, Francisco; Grötschel, Martin; Jünger, Michael; Reinelt, Gerhard: An application of combinatorial optimization to statistical physics and circuit layout design. In: *Oper. Res.*, volume 36(3):pp. 493–513, 1988.

[BGW03] Buchsbaum, Adam L.; Giancarlo, Raffaele; Westbrook, Jeffery R.: On finding common neighborhoods in massive graphs. In: *Theor. Comput. Sci.*, volume 299(1-3):pp. 707–718, 2003.

[Bol79] Bollobás, Bela: *Graph Theory, An Introductory Course*. Springer, New York, 1979.

[Bot93] Botafogo, Rodrigo A.: Cluster analysis for hypertext systems. In: *SIGIR '93: Proceedings of the 16th annual international ACM SIGIR conference on Research and development in information retrieval*, pp. 116–125. ACM, New York, NY, USA, 1993.

[BYKS02] Bar-Yossef, Ziv; Kumar, Ravi; Sivakumar, D.: Reductions in streaming algorithms, with an application to counting triangles in graphs. In: *SODA '02: Proceedings of the thirteenth annual ACM-SIAM symposium on Discrete algorithms*, pp. 623–632. Society for Industrial and Applied Mathematics, Philadelphia, PA, USA, 2002.

[CER] CERN: European Organisation for Nuclear Research, Geneva, Switzerland. http://public.web.cern.ch/public/Welcome.html.

[Cha00] Chazelle, Bernard: A minimum spanning tree algorithm with inverse-ackermann type complexity. In: *J. ACM*, volume 47(6):pp. 1028–1047, 2000.

[Che52] Chernoff, Herman: A measure of the asymptotic efficiency for tests of a hypothesis based on the sum of observations. In: *Annals of Mathematical Statistics*, volume 23:pp. 493–509, 1952.

[CJRT05] Chekuri, Chandra; Jansen, Klaus; Rolim, José D. P.; Trevisan, Luca, editors: *Approximation, Randomization and Combinatorial Optimization, Algorithms and Techniques, 8th International Workshop on Approximation Algorithms for Combinatorial Optimization Problems, APPROX 2005 and 9th InternationalWorkshop on Randomization and Computation, RANDOM 2005, Berkeley, CA, USA, August 22-24, 2005, Proceedings*, volume 3624 of *Lecture Notes in Computer Science*. Springer, 2005.

[CKMS06] Cormode, Graham; Korn, Flip; Muthukrishnan, S.; Srivastava, Divesh: Space- and time-efficient deterministic algorithms for biased quantiles over data streams. In: *PODS '06: Proceedings of the twenty-fifth ACM SIGMOD-SIGACT-SIGART symposium on Principles of database systems*, pp. 263–272. ACM, New York, NY, USA, 2006.

[CPV02] Cortes, Corinna; Pregibon, Daryl; Volinsky, Chris: Communities of interest. In: *Intell. Data Anal.*, volume 6(3):pp. 211–219, 2002.

[DEMR07] Demetrescu, Camil; Escoffier, Bruno; Moruz, Gabriel; Ribichini, Andrea: Adapting parallel algorithms to the W-stream model, with applications to graph problems. In: Kucera, Ludek; Kucera, Antonín, editors, *MFCS*, volume 4708 of *Lecture Notes in Computer Science*, pp. 194–205. Springer, 2007.

[DFR06] Demetrescu, Camil; Finocchi, Irene; Ribichini, Andrea: Trading off space for passes in graph streaming problems. In: *SODA '06: Proceedings of the seventeenth annual ACM-SIAM symposium on Discrete algorithm*, pp. 714–723. ACM, New York, NY, USA, 2006.

[Die05] Diestel, Reinhard: *Graph Theory*, volume 173 of *Graduate Texts in Mathematics*. Springer-Verlag, Heidelberg, 3rd edition, 2005.

[EGIN97] Eppstein, David; Galil, Zvi; Italiano, Giuseppe F.; Nissenzweig, Amnon: Sparsification—a technique for speeding up dynamic graph algorithms. In: *J. ACM*, volume 44(5):pp. 669–696, 1997.

[Elk07] Elkin, Michael: Streaming and fully dynamic centralized algorithms for constructing and maintaining sparse spanners. In: Arge, Lars; Cachin, Christian; Jurdzinski, Tomasz; Tarlecki, Andrzej, editors, *ICALP*, volume 4596 of *Lecture Notes in Computer Science*, pp. 716–727. Springer, 2007.

[FF56] Ford, Jr., Lester R.; Fulkerson, Delbert R.: Maximal flow through a network. In: *Canad. J. Math.*, volume 8:pp. 399–404, 1956.

[FKM+05a] Feigenbaum, Joan; Kannan, Sampath; Mcgregor, Andrew; Suri, Siddharth; Zhang, Jian: Graph distances in the streaming model: the value of space. In: *In ACM-SIAM Symposium on Discrete Algorithms*, pp. 745–754. 2005.

[FKM+05b] Feigenbaum, Joan; Kannan, Sampath; McGregor, Andrew; Suri, Siddharth; Zhang, Jian: On graph problems in a semi-streaming model. In: *Theor. Comput. Sci.*, volume 348(2):pp. 207–216, 2005.

[Gab90] Gabow, Harold N.: Data structures for weighted matching and nearest common ancestors with linking. In: *SODA '90: Proceedings of the first annual ACM-SIAM symposium on Discrete algorithms*, pp. 434–443. Society for Industrial and Applied Mathematics, Philadelphia, PA, USA, 1990.

[Gab95] Gabow, Harold N.: A matroid approach to finding edge connectivity and packing arborescences. In: *Selected papers of the 23rd annual ACM symposium on Theory of computing*, pp. 259–273. Academic Press, Inc., Orlando, FL, USA, 1995.

[Gab06] Gabow, Harold N.: Using expander graphs to find vertex connectivity. In: *J. ACM*, volume 53(5):pp. 800–844, 2006.

[GGI+02] Gilbert, Anna C.; Guha, Sudipto; Indyk, Piotr; Kotidis, Yannis; Muthukrishnan, S.; Strauss, Martin J.: Fast, small-space algorithms for approximate histogram maintenance. In: *STOC '02: Proceedings of the thiry-fourth annual ACM symposium on Theory of computing*, pp. 389–398. ACM, New York, NY, USA, 2002.

[GJ90] Garey, Michael R.; Johnson, David S.: *Computers and Intractability; A Guide to the Theory of NP-Completeness*. W. H. Freeman & Co., New York, NY, USA, 1990.

[GS06] Ganguly, Sumit; Saha, Barna: On estimating path aggregates over streaming graphs. In: *In International Symposium on Algorithms and Computation*, pp. 163–172. 2006.

[GW95] Goemans, Michel X.; Williamson, David P.: Improved approximation algorithms for maximum cut and satisfiability problems using semidefinite programming. In: *J. ACM*, volume 42(6):pp. 1115–1145, 1995.

[Hås01] Håstad, Johan: Some optimal inapproximability results. In: *J. ACM*, volume 48(4):pp. 798–859, 2001.

[HRR99] Henzinger, Monika R.; Raghavan, Prabhakar; Rajagopalan, Sridhar: Computing on data streams. In: *External memory algorithms*, pp. 107–118, 1999.

[Ind06] Indyk, Piotr: Stable distributions, pseudorandom generators, embeddings, and data stream computation. In: *J. ACM*, volume 53(3):pp. 307–323, 2006.

[JG05] Jowhari, Hossein; Ghodsi, Mohammad: New streaming algorithms for counting triangles in graphs. In: *Proceedings of the 11th Annual International Computing and Combinatorics Conference (COCOON '05)*. 2005.

[JLR00] Janson, Svante; Luczak, Tomasz; Rucinski, Andrzej: *Random Graphs*. John Wiley & Sons, New York, 2000.

[Kar72] Karp, Richard M.: Reducibility among combinatorial problems. In: Miller, R. E.; Thatcher, J. W., editors, *Complexity of Computer Computations*, pp. 85–103. Plenum Press, 1972.

[Kar94] Karger, David R.: Using randomized sparsification to approximate minimum cuts. In: *SODA '94: Proceedings of the fifth annual ACM-SIAM symposium on Discrete algorithms*, pp. 424–432. Society for Industrial and Applied Mathematics, Philadelphia, PA, USA, 1994.

[KKMO04] Khot, Subhash; Kindler, Guy; Mossel, Elchanan; O'Donnell, Ryan: Optimal inapproximability results for max-cut and other 2-variable CSPs? In: *FOCS '04: Proceedings of the 45th Annual IEEE Symposium on Foundations of Computer Science*, pp. 146–154. IEEE Computer Society, Washington, DC, USA, 2004.

[KN06] Kushilevitz, Eyal; Nisan, Noam: *Communication Complexity*. Cambridge University Press, New York, NY, USA, 2006.

[KRRT99] Kumar, Ravi; Raghavan, Prabhakar; Rajagopalan, Sridhar; Tomkins, Andrew: Trawling the web for emerging cyber-communities. In: *Computer Networks (Amsterdam, Netherlands: 1999)*, volume 31(11–16):pp. 1481–1493, 1999.

[LHC] LHC Computing Grid. http://lcg.web.cern.ch/LCG/.

[MAA06] Metwally, Ahmed; Agrawal, Divyakant; Abbadi, Amr El: An integrated efficient solution for computing frequent and top-k elements in data streams. In: *ACM Trans. Database Syst.*, volume 31(3):pp. 1095–1133, 2006.

[McG05] McGregor, Andrew: Finding graph matchings in data streams. In: Chekuri et al. [CJRT05], pp. 170–181.

[MMH97] Möhring, Rolf H.; Müller-Hannemann, Matthias: Complexity and modeling aspects of mesh refinement into quadrilaterals. In: *ISAAC '97: Proceedings of the 8th International Symposium on Algorithms and Computation*, pp. 263–272. Springer-Verlag, London, UK, 1997.

[MP78] Munro, J. Ian; Paterson, Mike S.: Selection and sorting with limited storage. In: *SFCS '78: Proceedings of the 19th Annual Symposium on Foundations of Computer Science*, pp. 253–258. IEEE Computer Society, Washington, DC, USA, 1978.

[MPD00] Monien, Burkhard; Preis, Robert; Diekmann, Ralph: Quality matching and local improvement for multilevel graph-partitioning. In: *Parallel Comput.*, volume 26(12):pp. 1609–1634, 2000.

[Mut05] Muthukrishnan, S.: Data streams: algorithms and applications. In: *Found. Trends Theor. Comput. Sci.*, volume 1(2):pp. 117–236, 2005.

[NI92] Nagamochi, Hiroshi; Ibaraki, Toshihide: A linear-time algorithm for finding a sparse k-connected spanning subgraph of a k-connected graph. In: *Algorithmica*, volume 7(5&6):pp. 583–596, 1992.

[Pap94] Papadimitriou, Christos M.: *Computational complexity*. Addison-Wesley, Reading, Massachusetts, 1994.

[Par08] Pardalos, Panos M.: Cliques, quasi-cliques and clique partitions in graphs, 2008.

[Pet99] Pettie, Seth: Finding minimum spanning trees in $O(m \cdot \alpha(m,n))$ time. Technical Report CS-TR-99-23, University of Texas, Austin, Texas, 1999. http://www.eecs.umich.edu/~pettie/papers/tr99-23.pdf.

[PR02] Pettie, Seth; Ramachandran, Vijaya: An optimal minimum spanning tree algorithm. In: *J. ACM*, volume 49(1):pp. 16–34, 2002.

[Pre99] Preis, Robert: Linear time 1/2-approximation algorithm for maximum weighted matching in general graphs. In: Meinel, Christoph; Tison, Sophie, editors, *STACS*, volume 1563 of *Lecture Notes in Computer Science*, pp. 259–269. Springer, 1999.

[PS04] Pettie, Seth; Sanders, Peter: A simpler linear time $2/3 - \epsilon$ approximation for maximum weight matching. In: *Inf. Process. Lett.*, volume 91(6):pp. 271–276, 2004.

[PT95] Poljak, Svatopluk; Tuza, Zsolt: Maximum cuts and largest bipartite subgraphs. In: *DIMACS series in Discrete Mathematics and Theoretical Computer Science*, volume 20:pp. 181–244, 1995.

[Ruh03] Ruhl, Jan M.: *Efficient Algorithms for New Computational Models*. Ph.D. thesis, Department of Electrical Engineering and Computer Science, Massachusetts Intstitute of Technology, 2003.

[Sch03] Schrijver, Alexander: *Combinatorial Optimization - Polyhedra and Efficiency*. Springer, 2003.

[SG76] Sahni, Sartaj; Gonzalez, Teofilo: P-complete approximation problems. In: *J. ACM*, volume 23(3):pp. 555–565, 1976.

[Tar83] Tarjan, Robert E.: *Data structures and network algorithms*. Society for Industrial and Applied Mathematics, Philadelphia, PA, USA, 1983.

[VH05] Vinkemeier, Doratha E. Drake; Hougardy, Stefan: A linear-time approximation algorithm for weighted matchings in graphs. In: *ACM Trans. Algorithms*, volume 1(1):pp. 107–122, 2005.

[Vit85] Vitter, Jeffrey S.: Random sampling with a reservoir. In: *ACM Trans. Math. Softw.*, volume 11(1):pp. 37–57, 1985.

[Woe04] Woeginger, Gerhard J.: Space and time complexity of exact algorithms: Some open problems (invited talk). In: Downey, Rodney G.; Fellows, Michael R.; Dehne, Frank K. H. A., editors, *IWPEC*, volume 3162 of *Lecture Notes in Computer Science*, pp. 281–290. Springer, 2004.

[Zel06] Zelke, Mariano: k-connectivity in the semi-streaming model. Technical report, Humboldt-University Berlin, 2006. http://arxiv.org/abs/cs/0608066.

[Zel07] Zelke, Mariano: Optimal per-edge processing times in the semi-streaming model. In: *Inf. Process. Lett.*, volume 104(3):pp. 106–112, 2007.

[Zel08] Zelke, Mariano: Weighted matching in the semi-streaming model. In: Albers, Susanne; Weil, Pascal, editors, *25th International Symposium on Theoretical Aspects of Computer Science (STACS 2008)*, pp. 669–680. 2008.

Die VDM Verlagsservicegesellschaft sucht für wissenschaftliche Verlage abgeschlossene und herausragende

Dissertationen, Habilitationen, Diplomarbeiten, Master Theses, Magisterarbeiten usw.

für die kostenlose Publikation als Fachbuch.

Sie verfügen über eine Arbeit, die hohen inhaltlichen und formalen Ansprüchen genügt, und haben Interesse an einer honorarvergüteten Publikation?

Dann senden Sie bitte erste Informationen über sich und Ihre Arbeit per Email an *info@vdm-vsg.de*.

Sie erhalten kurzfristig unser Feedback!

VDM Verlagsservicegesellschaft mbH
Dudweiler Landstr. 99
D - 66123 Saarbrücken
www.vdm-vsg.de

Telefon +49 681 3720 174
Fax   +49 681 3720 1749

Die VDM Verlagsservicegesellschaft mbH vertritt

Printed by Books on Demand GmbH, Norderstedt / Germany